RECOLLECTIONS OF THE GREAT WAR

THREE YEARS ON CAMPAIGN IN FRANCE AND FLANDERS WITH THE NORTHUMBERLAND FUSILIERS

RECOLLECTIONS OF THE GREAT WAR

THREE YEARS ON CAMPAIGN IN FRANCE AND FLANDERS WITH THE NORTHUMBERLAND FUSILIERS

FRANCIS BUCKLEY

Pen & Sword
MILITARY

This edition published in 2015 by

Pen & Sword Military
An imprint of
Pen & Sword Books Ltd.
47 Church Street
Barnsley
South Yorkshire
S70 2AS

This book was first published as 'Q.6.A and Other Places - Recollections of 1916, 1917, 1918'
by Spottiswoode, Ballantyne & Co. Ltd., London, 1920.

ISBN: 9781473833555

A CIP catalogue record for this book is available from the British Library.

Printed and bound in England
By CPI Group (UK) Ltd., Croydon, CR0 4YY

Pen & Sword Books Ltd. incorporates the imprints of Pen & Sword Aviation, Pen & Sword Family History, Pen & Sword Maritime, Pen & Sword Military, Pen & Sword Discovery, Pen & Sword Politics, Pen & Sword Atlas, Pen & Sword Archaeology, Wharncliffe Local History, Wharncliffe True Crime, Wharncliffe Transport, Pen & Sword Select, Pen & Sword Military Classics, Leo Cooper, The Praetorian Press, Claymore Press, Remember When, Seaforth Publishing and Frontline Publishing

For a complete list of Pen & Sword titles please contact
PEN & SWORD BOOKS LIMITED
47 Church Street, Barnsley, South Yorkshire, S70 2AS, England
E-mail: enquiries@pen-and-sword.co.uk
Website: www.pen-and-sword.co.uk

INTRODUCTION

IN THE FOLLOWING pages I have tried to set down as faithfully as I can some of the impressions which remain to me now of three years' service in France and Flanders.

I have naturally suppressed much of the grim and ghastly horrors that were shared by all in the fighting area. A narrative must be written from some point of view, and I have had to select my own. I regret that so much personal and trivial incident should appear. Perhaps some will be able to see through the gross egotistical covering and get a glimpse, however faint, of the deeds of deathless heroism performed by my beloved comrades - the officers and men of the 7th Northumberland Fusiliers, the officers and men of the 149th Infantry Brigade, the officers and men of the 50th Division.

The climax of the story is the battle on the Somme where so many dear friends have perished. The name is taken from a spot where a small party of the 7th N.F. did something long afterwards to avenge their fallen comrades.

Finally no criticism of the Higher Command is intended by anything that has been written. If such can be read between the lines, it is unintentional and a matter for sincere regret.

CONTENTS

NOTE

The following abbreviations are used:

B.H.Q.	-	Brigade Head-quarters.
C.C.S.	-	Casualty Clearing Station.
C.O.	-	Commanding Officer.
C.T.	-	Communication Trench.
D.A.Q.M.G.	-	Deputy-Assistant-Quartermaster-General.
D.H.Q.	-	Divisional Head-quarters.
F.A.	-	Field Ambulance.
H.Q.	-	Head-quarters.
L.-C.	-	Lance-Corporal.
N.C.O.	-	Non-commissioned Officer.
O.C.	-	Officer Commanding.
O.P.	-	Observation Post.
O.T.C.	-	Officers' Training Corps.
Q.M.	-	Quartermaster.
R.T.O.	-	Railway Transport Officer.
Y.M.C.A.	-	Young Men's Christian Association.

CHAPTER I
WHEN IT BEGAN

BEFORE THE WAR I was living in London, with chambers at Lincoln's Inn.

I was not surprised when the trouble started. Ever since 1904 it was reasonably clear to me that our country would have to fight the Germans or go under.

The days before we declared war on Germany were spent in London. During the last few of them it was as though a terrible thunderstorm was hanging overhead, ready to burst: gloom and foreboding on the faces of all. There is no doubt that most of our people were taken by surprise and that they were aghast at the sudden gathering of the war cloud. But when the stroke of fate fell and we were committed to the war, there was a curious sense of relief in many hearts. Better death and ruin than dishonour. A shameful peace or neutrality is for most Englishmen harder to bear than all the horrors of war. Besides, this struggle for freedom had to be fought out, though few can have foretold the cost.

I had been rejected for the Territorial Force by the Army authorities in 1908 on account of weak eyesight. I had therefore few hopes of better luck in August 1914. At first only trained men were enrolled at the Inns of Court O.T.C., and this went on for some months - till the nation in fact began to realise the size of its task. So after two or three vain attempts to find my way into the services, I had to be content with the truncheon and armlet of a special constable. With this force I had no special adventures, but I learnt a good deal about the Vine Street Police area, and about the electric power stations of the West End. Christmas Day was spent on duty in the streets, and Easter Day found me still there. Then something happened which decided my own little fate, as well perhaps as the fate of Europe. This was the sinking of the good ship *Lusitania* on May 7, 1915, under peculiarly barbarous and inhuman circumstances. Eventually it brought the Americans into the war, when they came to understand that the German people gloried in the deed of shame. As for me, it took me once again to the doors of the O.T.C. in Lincoln's Inn. If I could not go as an officer I would at least go into the ranks. But by this time the rush of officer recruits had died down, and they were not so particular about eyesight. So on May 10, 1915, I found myself in possession of a suit of khaki. It was second-or third-hand and an indifferent fit, but it enclosed a glad heart. The die was cast, and one little boat fairly launched on its perilous passage. Never have I had cause to lament this step. If it has brought me great troubles and anguish, it has also given peace of mind and the satisfaction of using to the full such energy as I possess. It took me out of the stifling heat of the town and gave me at least four years of an open-air life. For which God be thanked! If it did not bring much promotion or honour, it brought the friendship of real men, and a treasure greater than all the stars and ribbons in the world.

A recruit at the Inns of Court O.T.C. had nothing to fear from those in charge if he was willing to do his best. There was little boisterousness or horse-play among the recruits, the dark shadow was too close for that; and the spirit among my new comrades was one of great earnestness. For the first two or three weeks we were trained in Town near the H.Q. of the Battalion in Lincoln's Inn. After that recruits were sent on to the camp at Berkhamsted for field training. We were billeted on the local inhabitants. I stayed at the house of Mr. Charles Dipple, from whose family I received much kind hospitality. It was a sudden change for one who had spent the greater part of ten years in London chambers. And at Berkhamsted they worked you hard, almost to the last degree of physical endurance. Save once, during a dark two weeks in France, I have never before or since felt the same fatigue of body. Also the change of food was a little strange and startling at first. The drill and discipline could do nothing but good to a healthy man. The enthusiasm of nearly all was great, our chief idea being to get ready and out to France or elsewhere before the war should be over. Little did we know what the future had in store.

There is nothing much to tell of this part of one's experience. One of the most pleasant incidents was a fortnightly leave of thirty-six hours at the week-end, which I used to spend with my friends in Town. Night manoeuvres on Wednesdays and Fridays and guard duty were perhaps the most unpleasant part of our lot. Some would add the adjutant's parade on Saturday morning. But that was short, if not always sweet.

I had the good luck to win an unpaid lance-corporal's stripe towards the end of my stay, chiefly, I think, on account of a certain aptitude for drill, a clean rifle, and clean boots. Of this small achievement I was and still am a little proud.

I left the battalion on getting my commission with respect for the officers in charge of the training. The short experience in the ranks was to be of great value afterwards, when I came to deal for the first time as an officer with men in the ranks. It gave a certain sympathy with them and taught what to avoid. It was the custom of our C.O., Lieut.-Col. Errington, to give a few words of advice to those leaving the battalion to take up commissions. And I have never forgotten two of the principles which he urged upon us. One was the constant necessity for a soldier to deny himself in little things. The other was the idea that every officer in his own command, however small, had a duel to face with another officer in a similar position on the other side; and that in this duel the one that used his brain best would win. And so this embryo existence came to an end - a careless, happy time with no particular thought for the troubles ahead. In the middle of July 1915 I obtained a commission in the 3rd line Battalion of the 7th Northumberland Fusiliers, Territorials, supplying drafts to the 1st line battalion in France. I had no desire to display my ignorance of things military before a group of neighbours and possibly relations, so I applied for a commission, not in the Territorials of the West Riding Regiment, but in a north-country battalion of Territorials, with the 1st line fighting in France. The Territorial Force seemed to me most suitable for one who had no military career in view. And France, the land of old time romance and chivalry, gave a more urgent call than Egypt or the East. The choice of a unit, if one can be said to choose it, is fraught with greater consequences to oneself than might be supposed. I cannot say after a lapse of three years that the choice has proved unfortunate to me. It came about in this way. We were doing a rifle parade one day at Berkhamsted, when Lieut. Reynolds (N.F.) appeared with our company commander, Capt. Clarke, and asked for the names of any men who would like to join the 3rd line of the 7th N.F. The 1st line battalion, he said, had just been badly cut up in France, and we should be out there in four months perhaps, certainly in six months. That was all the information we had, but it was enough for me. A north-country territorial battalion and France in six months - those were the attractions. I had never spent more than one night in Northumberland and I knew of Alnwick only by name. It was therefore rather a step in the dark; but to one who was still ignorant of the meaning of a 'Brigade' or a 'Division' only general considerations could appeal. And so on July 30, 1915, I set off for Alnwick to join my battalion, with a new uniform and kit, with a somewhat nervous feeling inside, but with a determination to do my best.

CHAPTER II

THE MEN OF THE NORTH COUNTRY

I HAVE A great respect and admiration for the men of Northumberland. Especially for those who come from the country towns and villages, the farm-lands and mines in the northern parts of the county. As soldiers they have gained a name the world over, of which it would be idle for me to talk. A cold climate and a fighting ancestry that goes back many hundreds of years have produced some marked qualities in the race of Northumbrians to-day. There are few of them that are not true to type, few that you would not care to have as comrades in a tight corner. Their stubborn courage and contempt for danger have been proved again and again. The worse the outlook the more cheerful they seem to become. Sturdy independence is there, and for this allowance has to be made - slow to like and slow to change; if you are known as 'Mister' So-and-so, whatever your rank, you have won their respect. No better soldiers in the land can be found to hold or to fortify a position. But I doubt whether they have quite the same genius for the attack.[1] A certain lack of imagination, a certain want of forethought, have always, as it seems to me, been a handicap to these brave men when they attack. Again and again during an assault they have fallen in hundreds, they have shown themselves as willing to die in the open as in the trenches. But have they the wild fury that carries the Scot, the Irishman, or the Frenchman over 'impossible' obstacles? No, they are not an enthusiastic people, nor a very imaginative one. And these qualities are needed to press home a difficult attack. They are not

1. This criticism can of course be made of any troops of English nationality.

as a whole a quick or a very intelligent race. But for stark grim courage under the most awful surroundings they stand second to none. There is a streak of ruthlessness, too, in their dealings with the enemy; a legacy from the old Border wars with the Scots. They are quite ready, if need be, to take no prisoners. A hard and strong, but a very lovable race of men. Yes, I think all the world of the men of the north, although I am not blind to their faults. Taken as a whole no more handsome or manly set of men can be found in the British Isles.

The Northumbrian dialect is difficult to understand until you get the trick of it. And the trick of it is in the accent and intonation, and not so much in any peculiar form of words. They have a peculiar way of dropping their voices, too, which is sometimes disconcerting. But it is a clean wholesome language, undefined by the disgusting and childish obscenity which is too often a disgrace to other districts in England. It reminds me a little of the Scottish tongue, but rather more of the country speech in the northern parts of Yorkshire, but in some ways it is all its very own. It must indeed be one of the earliest surviving types of the Anglo-Saxon speech. I had no great difficulty in understanding it, but to this day I am sometimes puzzled to pick up what is said owing to that curious drop in the voice.

A word or two as well about the officers of the Northumberlands, meaning, of course, the natives of the county. For them as well as for the hardy miners and farmers of the north I have a very sincere respect and liking. Better comrades on the field of battle no man could wish for, better officers for a Territorial battalion it would be hard to find. Their unbending courage, their gallant bearing in danger, their cheerfulness and their care and thought for their men have been responsible in a great measure for the successes won by the Northumberland battalions and for the lamentable but noble sacrifices when success was denied. Gallant and devoted soldiers they have been, and well they have earned the love and admiration of their men. Always cheerful whatever was on foot, readiest of all to turn a danger passed into a jest. There could not be a better spirit in which to face the long delays and the bitter disappointments of the war. Two outstanding features in their character are, to my mind, practically universal, whatever form they happen to take. An inherent pugnacity, and a whole-hearted belief in and love of their county, which amounts to something more than clannishness. They know everything about every one in Northumberland, and with others they do not trouble themselves much. They do not talk about it like the Scots, but it is there all the same; and it has a profound influence on their actions and judgment. Within this sacred circle, into which no outlandish man can break, their pugnacity develops countless local feuds. And these feuds can be bitter enough, and I do not think I ever met a north-countryman without one. Generally there are two or three on foot at a time. One town against another, the men who did against the men who did not. Sometimes I have thought that these queer hereditary instincts, for such they undoubtedly are, have led the men of the north astray. The house has been divided against itself, justice has not been done, or it has been delayed, incompetence has been allowed to spread its blighting influence. In other words the love of their county and the strength of their local feuds have at times blinded the men of the north to the real interests of their country, when a united front and a concentration of the best effort available were absolutely necessary to get on with the war. To me the Northumbrian officer has been universally kind, and I have never had the least discourtesy or injustice from any of them, but many acts of kindness. But I have seen with regret on several occasions a loss of effort and strength through the divisions caused by prejudice. Thoroughly cheerful and a generous and charming comrade, much given to hospitality, I do not think the Northumbrian officer is always a very brilliant person intellectually. There are many notable exceptions, but they are notable enough to establish the impression.

Beyond these general observations it would be unwise - and I do not intend - to enter into the domestic history of any battalion or brigade. Better comrades one could not have, and a nobler and more devoted body of men I have yet to meet.

CHAPTER III

ALNWICK

A SHORT SKETCH of my stay at Alnwick may not be out of place. For though it did not seem very adventurous at the time it had a great influence on my subsequent career, both in France and afterwards. It is a most romantic spot, with one of the finest castles in England. The heather hills run down through corn-land towards the seashore; and the general features of the countryside reminded me much of my own home in the West Yorkshire hills. The curious battlements and gates in the town and the monuments outside tell of a time when it was one of England's front line posts against the raiding Scots. It seemed to me to be a fitting spot to train men for the wars.

When I arrived at the end of July 1915 the H.Q. of the 3rd line battalion were at the Star Hotel in Fenkle Street - very comfortable but rather expensive quarters. Only a few of the officers had arrived as yet. Just a few new-comers like myself, very green and raw, and about four or five officers of the 1st line battalion who had returned wounded from France. These latter had for the most part been wounded at the battle of St. Julien in April 1915, during the 2nd Battle of Ypres. They were now discharged from hospital and attached to the draft battalion for training before going out once more. They were very friendly and nice to the new-comers; and indeed we looked upon them quite as veterans, although their active service in France had not exceeded a few days. Capt. J. Welch, Lieuts. J.W. Merivale, E. Nixon, and E. Fenwicke Clennell became special friends of mine, and I am grateful for many acts of kindness from them both then and later on abroad. The men of the battalion, also raw recruits and wounded men returned from hospital, were quartered in the houses in the town. The O.C. battalion was Major (afterwards Lieut.-Colonel and Brevet Colonel)

J.J. Gillespie, T.D., and the Adjutant Capt. W.A.C. Darlington. The C.O. was a man of great personality, so much so that he is one of the best known and most talked of persons in the Northumberlands. A great organiser and a hard worker, who generally got his own way with small and great, he has done much to make the drafts efficient. I was lucky to find favour in his eyes, and our relations were always friendly.

We had as near neighbours in Alnwick the Brigade of Tyneside Scottish, who were encamped in the Pastures near the Castle, as fine a body of men as you could wish to see. After staying for a while at the Star our battalion moved out to Moorlaws Camp and we remained there under canvas till the middle of October. In the meantime I was lent for about five days to the 21st Provisional Battalion N.F., a home service battalion, who were encamped at Cambois ('Cammis') on the sea-coast. This was like a picnic for me, for all the officers there treated me kindly and did not work me hard. One night I volunteered for night duty and had the experience of visiting the sentries (all with loaded rifles) at the various posts along the shore. Shortly after returning to Alnwick I was sent, on September 2, to the Army School of Signalling and Bombing at Tynemouth, and went through the Bombing course, which lasted about a week. So primitive were the arrangements, even at this date, that we were only taught how to improvise grenades out of old jam tins, and how to fire them out of iron pipes as trench-mortar bombs. We were indeed allowed to handle precious specimens of the famous No. 3 (Hales) and No. 5 (Mills), but there were not enough available for live practice. The West Spring Thrower had not arrived, but I saw a trench catapult in action; and some dummy Stokes bombs were fired off for us to see. At this course there was an examination, and I got a first-class certificate as a grenade instructor, an event which had considerable influence on my career in France, as will appear later on. When I got back to Alnwick I found the battalion under canvas at Moorlaws. Here I became 'grenadier officer' to the battalion, and I had daily classes of men who had volunteered to become bombers, or 'grenadiers' as they were then called.

Live practice was carried out entirely with improvised bombs, old jam tins and black powder. But we procured a certain number of dummies of Nos. 1 and 5 to practise throwing. Major N.I. Wright (who had returned wounded) took a great interest in our proceedings and had some dummy grenades made for us. A gallant soldier with hard service in South Africa and the Great War, he has always been a good friend to me. I went on with the bombing till about October 20, when the battalion returned to Alnwick and went into wooden huts in the Pastures. The officers were billeted at a house called 'Alnbank,' a mansion some little distance from the men's quarters. After this move I was appointed Company Commander to C Company, a newly formed company with only raw recruits in it. My second in command was Lieut. Joseph Robinson, a dear friend, who had come all the way from the Argentine, and whom I first met at the O.T.C. at Berkhamsted. He was known as 'Strafer Robinson' on account of being physical drill instructor, and a pretty exacting one. I found the recruits in C Company most willing and anxious to learn their job; and they never gave me much trouble either in orderly room or on parade.

I was kindly treated by every one at Alnwick. My stay there has only pleasant memories. Major the Hon. Arthur Joicey, who had returned from the 1st line, gave me several glorious days after partridges at Longhirst. The number of these birds so far north fairly astonished me. The doctors' families in Alnwick were also very kind and hospitable to all our officers. Mrs. Scott Jackson, the wife of the Colonel of the 1st line battalion, could not do enough for us; and many happy evenings have been spent at her house; notably a great New Year's Eve party for all the officers, just before I left for the front. I took part in a Rugby football match, the first time for eleven years. The 3rd line 7th N.F. succeeded in defeating the reserve battalion of the Tyneside Scottish, largely through the prowess of 2nd-Lieut. McNaught at half-back. There was rather a pleasant institution towards the end of my stay - namely, a meeting of the senior officers for dinner every Wednesday evening at the Plough Inn. They did you well there, and it was a pleasant change from the mess dinner.

About January 3, 1916, I was warned to proceed with a small draft of officers to the front. Four of us were to go, and I was delighted to find myself one of those selected. After a splendid farewell dinner with the officers of the battalion on January 4, I left the same night for London to spend my final leave.

CHAPTER IV

THE JOURNEY OUT

ON MONDAY, JANUARY 10, 1916, I left England with three other officers, bound for the Base Camp at Havre. My companions were 2nd-Lieuts. Peters, O. Clarke, and Gregson. My final purchases at Southampton included an extra haversack and some morphia pills. The latter had been strongly recommended for certain kinds of wounds and they were still sold without a prescription.[2] The journey across the Channel was done at night. The transport left port about 8 P.M. and steaming slowly without lights reached Le Havre about 5 A.M. next morning.

My last view of England was the dreary wet dock, and later on a few distant and receding lights. Though we got into port at 5 A.M. we were not allowed to leave the vessel till 8 A.M. But, at last, as a cold and cheerless morning was breaking, I stepped ashore and set foot for the first time on foreign soil. We soon found an hotel (? Hôtel de Normandy) where they understood the English language and some of our ways, and we got breakfast in the English fashion. After a look round the shops and a shave in a small establishment in a side street, we reported at a large office in the town. Here we signed our names in a large register, and were given directions to proceed to a Camp, some distance from the town, where reinforcements for the 7th N.F. were collected and accommodated till they could be sent 'up the line.' Our stay here was a short one, for which I was thankful. They did not seem at all pleased to see us; it seems we had arrived a few days later than had been expected, and the Camp Commandant appeared to think it was our fault. We left Le Havre next day without having tasted the joys of the 'Bull Ring' or

2. Fortunately I never had occasion to use them.

any other educational entertainment prepared for those staying on at the Camp. The train started about midnight, and like most troop trains in France moved along in a leisurely, dignified manner, with frequent stops and long waits between the stations. When we did arrive at Rouen, which was about midday on Thursday, we had to change. And feeling unrefreshed by our night in the train, we spent the time resting at an hotel instead of seeing the sights. But it is a fine looking old town and would be worth visiting in more peaceful times.

We left Rouen again at night and wandered along in the same dilatory fashion, arriving at Hazebrouck and eventually at Poperinghe.

The latter was railhead for the Ypres Salient. It was not surprising then to find the houses near the railway station looking shattered from the shells and bombs that had been aimed at the station. We had tea with the Y.M.C.A., who had with their usual dauntlessness selected a house close to the station. It had been struck by a bomb a few nights before, and there was a hole in the roof and in the ceiling and floor of one of the rooms; but I understood that no one had been hurt by the explosion. These shattered houses and the distant sound of gun fire, which we first heard about Hazebrouck, were the first signs of war that we noticed. After a long wait a limber arrived at the station to take ourselves and our valises to the camp of the 7th N.F. at Ouderdom. It was not really a very long journey, I believe, but it seemed so to us after our long and wearisome journey in the train.

To make matters worse the military police made us take a roundabout road, and the driver lost his way. Of course a limber is not quite the vehicle you would select for comfort, especially over roads that are stony or pavé. The German flare lights could be clearly seen all the way, and they seemed to be on three sides of us. A most brilliant and interesting sight the first time you see it.

Eventually we reached the camp at Ouderdom. It was called 'Canada Huts' and consisted of a cluster of wooden huts erected just off a narrow muddy road. At one time I am told, the mud was thigh deep; but now duck boards had been laid down, and though decidedly muddy the camp was quite passable. When we arrived it was quite late, and we found the camp in total darkness and every one asleep. But some of the batmen (or officers' servants) were roused, and they not only showed us a place to sleep in, but got us some tea and a scratch meal, very welcome after our uncomfortable ride from the station. What wonderful people these batmen are! Always so cheery and good to their officers. Inside the huts we found wooden bunks in two tiers round three sides and also a wooden table and forms in the middle. Not much room to move about perhaps, but fairly dry and warm. After two sleepless nights in the train we did not need rocking.

We found that we had arrived just in time to go with the battalion to the front line trenches next day. For the battalion had just spent three days in the rest area and was due to take over the line on the fourth day. There was not much time, therefore, to get acquainted with our fellow officers or to learn much about the platoons to which we were assigned. Several of the officers we had known well at home in the 3rd line battalion at Alnwick, and Major N.I. Wright and Capt. J. Welch and Lieuts. J.W. Merivale and Fenwicke Clennell were old friends. Also we had already met our new battalion commander Lieut.-Col. G. Scott Jackson at Alnwick when he was last on leave. It was nice to be greeted by friendly faces when our trials were so soon to begin.

The last few hours before going back to the line are always rather dreary and unprofitable, spent chiefly in packing up and deciding what to leave behind. Valises of course were left behind with all 'spare parts' in the Q.M.'s stores. But in winter a fairly heavy load of things was necessary, and the weather was wet and stormy. We had no steel helmets in these days and no gas box-respirators, only two cloth respirators of little weight. I found myself in charge of No. 4 Platoon in A Company, of which Capt. H.R. Smail was commander. There were two other 2nd-Lieuts. in the company besides myself. The fighting strength of a company did not much exceed 100 men, if as many.

Before we left Canada Huts, I was provided with a batman, coming of course from A Company. And a good fellow he was and much I owe to him. He has looked after me continuously from the day after I arrived until he was demobilised on December 24, 1918 - nearly three years.

A miner from Ashington, wounded at St. Julien in April 1915, he had rejoined the battalion some months before in France. At a later stage I had to rely much on his skill as a cook. A wonderfully cheerful person and a smart and handy man at improvising little comforts for me. His name was William Critchlow.

CHAPTER V

HILL 60

WHEN IT WAS beginning to get dark the battalion formed up in the road and the roll was called over. At last we set off slowly, squelching through the mud on the wet roads, the rain pouring down unceasingly. We soon struck the pavé road that runs through Dickebusch, a long straggling village, still fairly intact and occupied by Belgian civilians. It was shelled now and again but not severely. When we reached this place, the battalion opened out considerably, platoons keeping 200 yards apart; a precaution necessary on roads that were periodically shelled at night. After plodding along for some time we reached the Café Belge, a mere ruin now, but a well-known halting place for troops on the march. Here we turned off to the right and left the pavé road which runs on to Ypres, and after this the roads were much more difficult to travel. Shell holes were frequent and generally full of water, so that in the dark it was only too easy to stumble into them. 'Shell-hole on the right,' 'Shell-hole on the left,' 'Shell-hole in the middle,' 'Keep to your right' were being passed back continually. Progress was slow of course under these conditions and with the heavy loads that we all carried. But it was all so novel to me that I had not a moment to feel dull or depressed. After a time we reached the notorious 'Shrapnel Corner' and turned towards 'Transport Farm,' for we were bound for trenches at Hill 60. This place was of course famous for the British attack in 1915, and for the German counter-attack with gas a little later on which was all too successful. It was also notorious for being one of the hottest corners of the British front. Owing to their vantage ground on the hill the enemy had little difficulty in sniping and shelling our trenches effectively.

As we approached Transport Farm I came for the first time under indirect rifle fire. A number of bullets fired at our trenches carried over and landed not far from the roads at the back. Though rather alarming in the dark to one unaccustomed to them, they seldom did much damage. Occasionally a man or two got wounded during these reliefs. Our company turned to the left again near Zillebeke railway station, and then struck off the road and reached the mouth of a C.T. which led after about a hundred yards to the support trenches.

A glance at the official plan of the trenches at Hill 60 will give some idea of the extraordinary place it was. Whilst the German line ran solid along the top of the ridge, there were two complete gaps in the British fire trenches between Hill 60 and Mount Sorrel on the left. On paper it looks as if there were nothing to stop the German from walking across and behind our lines whenever he chose. But I imagine that these empty spaces were covered by machine-gun posts, and that the artillery were ready to deal with any attempt of that sort. Another feature of the place was the awful nature of the ground outside the trenches. It was a morass filled with partially buried bodies - that is, partially buried by nature in the ooze and mud. During a dense mist about seventy identity discs were recovered from the ground behind our support lines. And it was worse in front between the opposing trenches. It was not likely, then,

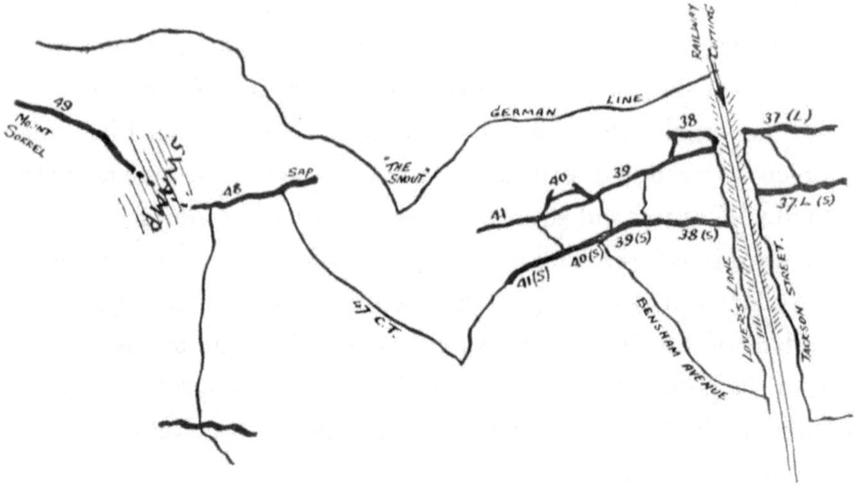

Hill 60. - Official Map, March 1916.

that the German would wish to press us farther down the hill, at any rate for tactical purposes.

A Company had two platoons in the front line trench 41, some 100 yards from the enemy, and two platoons in a support line called '41 support.' The trenches themselves were well-built and revetted with sand bags, and dry enough even during the wettest weather. We had in these days only small shelters - the deep dugout was unknown. The three subalterns in A Company took turns at duty in the trenches, four hours on and eight hours off, night and day. The duty consisted chiefly of visiting the sentries every hour, and keeping a general look-out, and seeing that the trench rules were obeyed. A good deal of rifle fire went on at night. Sentries on either side would exchange shots, and an occasional machine-gun would open out. At close range the bullets make a curious crack as they pass overhead. Being tall and having been warned of the efficiency of the German sniper, I had to walk in most of the trenches with a bend in the back, which soon became tiring.

On Sunday, January 16, I had a decidedly lively time for my first day in the trenches. It was always said that the Germans got a fresh supply of ammunition at the week-end, and Sunday was scarcely ever a day of rest. However that may be, this Sunday was the worst day I had for some time. After sending over a few small howitzer shells, the German field-guns sent periodical showers of shells, 'whizz-bangs' we called them, on to the support trench and C.T.

This went on all morning, and whilst the shoot lasted they came over in a perfect stream. After a quieter afternoon a regular trench battle opened out at night, rifle grenades and bombs being freely exchanged, and a number of trench-mortar bombs - 'sausages and rum jars' - coming over from the enemy's trenches. Eventually our heavy guns opened out with lively retaliation and the enemy quietened down. Rather a big dose to get the first day in the trenches, when everything was so strange and new. However I was assured that it was not an 'average' day even on Hill 60, but something like an organised shoot. One of the features of the place was the number and size of the rats; they looked the size of rabbits as they scuttered along the trenches at night. Another was the awful taste of the water we got to drink. It was boiled and it was turned into strong tea, but it had a most indescribably horrible taste. The food, on the other hand, was excellent and plenty of it. In the light of subsequent rations these were indeed the days of plenty. Owing to the kindness of some friends of the battalion in England, both officers and men were supplied with sheep-skin coats or jackets which were wonderfully good in keeping out the cold at night. 'Stand-to' was a regular institution of trench warfare, both an hour before dark and an hour before dawn. Naturally the latter was the more trying, but at this time the rum ration was served out; and it certainly prevented you from being frozen stiff and enabled you to get to sleep again if your duties did not keep you to the trenches. A very curious life in the trenches, a very small world but every bit of it packed full of interest and novelty to me. From the trenches, if you looked backwards, there was a splendid view of Ypres, with its shattered spires and houses, still a beautiful grey ruin, even in death. I was destined to have a much closer acquaintance with it later. Beyond the usual rounds of shelling on both sides nothing of particular interest happened during the next three days. On the evening of January 19 we were relieved by a company of the 5th N.F. (Capt. North M.C.), and moved out after dark for a short rest in close support.

My career as a platoon commander in the trenches was a short one, for as it happened that was my first and last experience as such. We moved out and back for about a mile, eventually reaching a house called Blauwpoorte Farm.[3] It was not a bad place then, and was not shelled, though at night the bullets used to rattle round if you walked abroad. Here on the second day I took a small party of men, as a working party, to the shelters at the 'Sunken Road,' rather nearer the line. I think we were engaged in clearing the road of mud and generally cleaning up. On the way there I saw some rather humourous notices stuck up at various points. 'This is a dangerous spot.' It was kindly meant no doubt, but on

3. Lieut. F.B. Cowen, a very cheery machine-gun officer, also 7th N.F., had his quarters here.

the whole no part of the Salient afforded much of a rest-cure, and it was practically all under direct observation of the enemy. We existed simply through his forbearance.

On January 22, 1916, I became bombing officer to the battalion, or, as it was then called, 'grenadier officer.' My predecessor had had bad luck, getting his hand shattered by the accidental explosion of a detonator. Accordingly I was sent to see Sergt. W. Moffat, the battalion bombing sergeant, in order to pick up what I could of the routine at so short a notice. Sergt. Moffat was a short withered man with sandy hair, a quiet manner, but a cheery twinkle in his eye. He had served in the South African war; and had been mentioned in despatches for good bombing work during a German attack at Hooge. A most conscientious and hard-working fellow, with a passion for all sorts of bombs. I could not have fallen into better hands. He was an admirable instructor and assistant, and knew all there was to be known about trench routine. I could see he was universally respected in the battalion. He was a Salvation Army man at home, and wore their red woollen jersey under his tunic. Much do I owe him and much do I still lament his untimely end.

Capt. Smail returned to England about this time, leaving me his woolly coat, a priceless parting gift. Capt. J. Welch came to command A Company and a cheerier fellow surely never existed. I was glad to accept his offer of messing with A Company. There never was a dull moment at mess when Welch presided.

We went back to Hill 60 for four days on January 23. I cannot remember much of this stay in the line, and nothing special happened. I was too busy learning all I could of the routine of the trenches and locating and checking bomb stores. I had to visit all the trenches held by the battalion, and thus got the chance of making the acquaintance of the other Company commanders, Capt. H. Liddell (B Coy.), Capt. C. Davies (C Coy.) and Capt. G.F. Ball, M.C., (D Coy.). I remember being asked by our Brigadier-General Clifford to explain some part of a derelict West Spring Thrower in the cutting at Hill 60 (I had never even seen one before) and being saved by the timely intervention of Sergt. Moffat.

On January 27 we were relieved and went back to Canada Huts for a rest of four days. Oh, that first rest out of the trenches! The accommodation was poor enough seen in the light of home comforts, but what a palace of rest and refreshment it seemed to me then, and how quickly the time passed. I had to practise the bombers (nineteen from each company) in throwing dummy grenades each morning on the mud flat (it was once a field) outside the huts. In order to stimulate keenness I organised a competition and gave one franc each day as a prize for the best score. I soon found out who were the most expert throwers.

We had a Y.M.C.A. hut close to the camp, and it was interesting to drop in and have a chat with the men in charge and a cup of cocoa. There was an old gentleman there, in command, who was rightly proud of being the civilian nearest to the front line. He displayed to us with great pride a souvenir found in Ypres, the huge base of a 17-inch shell - it was almost too heavy for one man to lift. We had our Church Service and our concerts in the marquee attached to the Y.M.C.A. hut.

Most of the officers got leave to go to Poperinghe during these rests out of the line, but I never went there myself. There was an attraction there in the 'Fancies,' a fine concert party, many of whose songs I learnt at second hand.

CHAPTER VI

MOUNT SORREL AND CANNY HILL

WHEN WE WENT up the line again on January 31, it was to Mount Sorrel, on the north of Hill 60. Here we had a good set of trenches, but they were practically cut off from our trenches at Hill 60 by a swamp. Through the swamp ran a watery sort of drain about four feet deep. It was the old front line, now waterlogged and quite untenable. Although the drain was not held by day, a patrol of bombers used to pass along it at intervals during the night. And it was part of my duties to wade through it every night. This was not a pleasant job, because you could not show a light and the mud smelt abominably. We were provided, however, with rubber boots reaching up to the thigh, so we did not get very wet. The officers of A Company occupied an 'elephant' shelter just behind the support line. All its occupants were killed by a shell bursting in the doorway, just two days after we had left these trenches. I first met Lieut. W. Keene here. He was the Brigade Grenadier officer and had the supervision of all bombing arrangements in the Brigade area, besides being responsible for the supply of grenades. I always found him friendly and encouraging, and I was glad to learn anything he could tell me. He asked me to send in a daily report to B.H.Q.; and I have kept the copies of these reports to this day.

During this stay in the trenches the Germans stuck up a notice board with the following legend: *Attention Gentlemen*, and below in German, 'If you send over one more trench-mortar bomb you will get strafed in the neck.'

On February 3 we were relieved and A Company stayed four days in the railway cutting at Hill 60 in close support. The second day I went with Capt. Welch and Lieut. Greene to the trenches north of Mount Sorrel which were called Canny Hill. That journey was full of incident, we seemed to be shelled or bombed all the way to Mount Sorrel and back, and Capt. Welch has often humourously suggested that I was the Jonah. It also meant crossing the dismal swamp in daylight, and how we did it without being seen and shot I really do not know. During our stay in the cutting I explored the old broken trenches behind our support line at Hill 60, and found a fine dump of English bombs of early types. I spent quite a long time drawing their teeth. One little incident I remember at this spot. About 1 A.M. an elderly R.E. officer came into our shelter, and told us in a voice shaking with joyful emotion that he had just blown up a German counter-mine which had been threatening our mine galleries at Hill 60.

On February 8 we marched back to Canada Huts, and had another four days' rest. This time the bombers carried out a good deal of live practice with Mills bombs at some bombing-pits about half a mile from Canada Huts. It was my first experience of the sort; but Sergt. Moffat kept me up to the procedure at the firing-pit. Also it was the first time I had the chance of throwing a live Mills bomb myself. On February 12 we were due to take over the trenches at Canny Hill, and I went up early and by myself, riding to Café Belge and thence on foot to Hill 60, Mount Sorrel, and so on to Sanctuary Wood. It was a long way round but I knew no other way. My dugout was in the wood, rather far from the front line and from the H.Q. of A Company in Davison Street. Our front line trenches were about quarter of a mile away from the German front line, but there were signs that the Germans were digging a forward trench along a hedge about 200 yards away from our front. This activity gave the Staff some uneasiness, and considerable interest was taken in these forward workings. I went out with Capt. Welch for a short visit in that direction the first night, but we saw nothing of interest. The next night Capt. Welch brought back a revetting stake from the new German trench. I believe it was on February 13 that the Germans attacked and took the 'Bluff,' some trenches south-west of Hill 60. About 3.30 P.M. our own trenches were bombarded for about two hours continuously with field artillery, and a lot of pieces were blown out of the top of our trenches, but no infantry attack developed. After this a small mine was blown up under our old trenches at Hill 60 and a platoon was wiped out there. But an attempt by the Germans to occupy the crater was frustrated through the initiative of a machine-gun officer. I saw and felt the shock of this mine going up, and a wonderful sight it was in the evening light. The shelling went on for some time after dark, whilst to our right our artillery thundered away in support of several fruitless attempts to recapture the lost trenches at the 'Bluff.'

On February 14 I was told to organise a series of bombing parties, one from each company, to visit the German advanced trench at different times during the night and if possible to bomb German parties working there. I decided to accompany the first party, from A Company, between 8 and 10 P.M. Sergt. Dorgan, an experienced patroller, went with me, also L.-C. Lowes, Ptes. Austin and Gibson, and two other bombers. As it was very wet, I had a sandbag taken by each man to lie down on. The scheme was to creep right up to the new trench near the hedge, and await the arrival of the German working-party. So we crept out along the wet ground and got to the trench, which was about two feet deep. We found no one there, and Pte. Austin went on into the hedge to keep a look-out. In the hedge were found a German sniper's plate, a steel shield with a loop-hole in it, and a German entrenching tool, like a small spade. These were at once annexed. Then we lay down again on the sandbags and waited with eyes and ears straining for about an hour. But no Germans came, though we had one warning from our sentry to get ready to fire. After that, cold and thoroughly soaked, we returned in triumph with the sandbags and our spoils, which we placed in our own trench. The other parties went out later but found no Germans at work. Possibly the wet night or the battle on our right prevented them from coming out to work that night. The object of these forward trenches was afterwards apparent, when four months later the Germans attacked and took Mount Sorrel. On February 16 we were relieved and went back into support for four days. I have forgotten where we went, but I think it was to the Canal Dugouts not far from Swan Château.

On February 20 we returned to the same trenches at Canny Hill and held them for five days. The first night in, Capt. Welch was badly wounded through the shoulder whilst bringing in a wounded man who had been hit whilst outside wiring. He was a great loss to the battalion, and was sadly missed by the men as well as by the officers. It now turned very cold, and we had a fall of snow several inches deep. This made it difficult for parties to work in the trenches without being spotted. I had an unpleasant experience of this. I was looking for an emplacement for a grenade-rifle stand, and I selected a likely-looking spot just behind the front line. Then I brought a party of bombers to dig the place out. We had not thrown out five shovelfuls of earth before a shell came whistling just over our heads. Fortunately I dispersed the party at once along the trench. Then the fun began. Shells came whizzing in all round the unlucky spot, till a direct hit right in the middle of it apparently satisfied the German gunners and the storm ceased. After that I chose another place farther along the trench where no digging was required.

On February 25 we left Canny Hill and went back to Canada Huts. On this occasion we had to make rather a detour to allow the troops of the 3rd Division to use the roads; and in so doing we passed Ypres railway station.

On March 1 we moved into the support dugouts at Transport Farm, called Railway Dugouts. We were told to expect a bombardment by our guns that night, as the 'Bluff' was to be attacked and retaken early next day. The bombers of the 7th N.F. spent some time detonating grenades by candlelight in the bomb store at Transport Farm. Sure enough there was a terrific bombardment for half an hour. It was the first of the kind that I had seen, and I believe that at least 500 guns of all calibres were collected for the occasion. The whole of the landscape seemed to be alight, every hedge flickering with flame; whilst away towards the 'Bluff' there was a sullen red glare where our shells were bursting. Nothing further happened that night. But at dawn next morning the 3rd Division attacked the 'Bluff' without bombardment and surprised the garrison, taking many prisoners and recapturing the lost trenches and some more ground besides. I saw one or two droves of prisoners coming back past Bedford House, the first time I had seen any live Boches. The bombardment by our guns started again soon after the attack, and our guns kept up a slow rate of fire all day. In reply the German heavy guns shelled the back areas freely, especially the road past Transport Farm, and we got a few shells near the railway. We got orders to take over the trenches at Mount Sorrel the same night. I left with a party of bombers soon after 1 P.M., going along a C.T. to Sanctuary Wood and then back through the trenches to Mount Sorrel.

We found the trenches in a sad mess. That morning there had been a demonstration with all arms along this part of the front, and the enemy had naturally retaliated and done a lot of damage. To increase our troubles it became very cold, and the snow fell inches deep. But there was no more shelling on either side for the next week. Apart from sniping, which was assisted by the snow, we were left in peace to bale out the mud and repair the trenches. This cold snap caused a lot of sickness, and it was not improved by our having to hold these trenches for over a week - a long time under such wintry conditions. At last, on March 9, we were relieved and moved back to some dugouts near Bedford House. Here we stayed for some days, taking working-parties up to Hill 60 at night, from 7 P.M. to 1 A.M. One night we were shelled off the roads, and had to come back with nothing done. Another time I took a party to mend a breach in the front line at Hill 60. I think we went back to Canada Huts about March 16 - at any rate we had a longer rest than usual. Sir Douglas Haig came over to Canada Huts to inspect the battalion. Amongst other things he inspected A Company who were drawn up in their hut, 2nd-Lieut. Gregson and myself being the subalterns there in charge. The General spoke to Gregson first, and asked him how long he had been out. He replied: 'January 14, sir' - meaning January 14, 1916. His reply was, however, taken to mean 'January 1914,' and quite a little discussion took place, which amused me much, as Gregson stuck to his point. Afterwards the General came round to my end of the hut and asked me how long I had been out. 'January '16, sir,' I replied. 'That's all right,' he said, 'well, I wish you the best of luck.' There was an amused twinkle in his kind sympathetic face, as I was still half-smiling over his little controversy with Gregson.

After this we moved off to another rest camp not far away, for a few days. On March 24 we were due to take over the trenches at Hill 60 again for three days. I went up early in the day and 'took over' the various bombing arrangements. The trenches now included some on the south side of the Railway Cutting, and I had my dugout there in the top of a small hillock called the 'Mound.' From 7.30 P.M. to 10 P.M. that night the trenches and Cutting were heavily bombarded, but the relief was not much delayed. The 7th N.F., however, had great luck in having only two men wounded whilst coming in. They were unfortunate casualties, it is true, 2nd-Lieut. J.H.C. Swinney[4] and Sergt. Dorgan, both good men and a loss to the battalion. The next three days were bad days for us. The battalion had over fifty casualties, much above the average. Four days in the line generally gave about seven or eight casualties. On March 25 British mines were exploded at St. Eloi, and the mine craters were occupied by the 3rd Division. The explosion took place just before dawn, about a mile or more to the south, but it woke me all of a shake. I thought at first that I was going to tumble down into the Cutting the ground heaved and rocked so much. The German heavy artillery took the precaution of bombarding our part of the front, and caused many casualties and much damage in the front line. The whole of C Company batmen were killed by a shell, and 2nd-Lieut. Burt, a new arrival but an old friend, was also killed. Poor lad, he was always certain that he would be killed as soon as he got out to France! I saw in the trenches a pile of our dead, three or four deep, waiting for removal to the rear. The shelling was severe at times during the next two days. Lieut. Platt, a forward observing officer of the 50th Divisional Artillery and a well known and welcome figure in the trenches, was killed by a shell just below my own dugout. We had cause, indeed, to remember our last visit to Hill 60. During this visit I first met some Canadian officers who were looking over the line before taking it over from the 50th Division.

---

4. A special friend, who unhappily was killed at Wancourt in 1917.

On March 27 we were relieved and I went back with A Company to some dugouts near Bedford House. Our first day there we were shelled out of these dugouts and had to take refuge for a time in Bedford House. A Belgian battery had just arrived close to us, and unfortunately they gave the position away. In the afternoon I went a long round to various reserve bomb stores to check the stores. Next night I paid a last visit to the Cutting at Hill 60 with a working-party. Second-Lieut. E.W. Styles was also there on a similar job.

He had just come out; and being anxious to see something of the famous Hill 60 trenches he went off by himself into the front line, and, I suppose, asked various questions of the sentries. Anyway, when next I saw him he was coming back down the Cutting followed at an interval by a sentry with a fixed bayonet, who asked me if I knew who he was. My reply was no doubt disappointing to the soldier, who thought he had really captured a spy this time, and earned his two weeks' leave - the reward for arresting a spy.

On March 29, before leaving the area, I acted as guide to some Canadian troops, from Café Belge to the Canal Dugouts. They seemed to be fine fellows and well up to strength in all their companies. The same night our battalion went back to Scottish Lines at Ouderdom, but we moved back to Canada Huts next day.

CHAPTER VII

KEMMEL

ON MARCH 31 I rode over with various company officers to Kemmel, and we looked over the trenches H2-K1 below Wytschaete Ridge. We were to take over this part of the line from the Canadians in two days' time. It was once a quiet spot, and I think we were sent there for that reason. But we soon found that we had come out of the frying-pan only to go into the fire. The battle that was still raging at St. Eloi about a mile to the north was destined to alter the character of the once peaceful Kemmel area. I had now changed my mess. All the old officers of A Company had disappeared since I first joined the battalion; so I accepted an invitation from Capt. G.F. Ball to join D Company mess. I was glad to do this, for not only was Capt. Ball the kindest and best of fellows, but there were old friends there - 2nd-Lieuts. Peters and J. Robinson - whom I knew well at Alnwick.

On April 1 the battalion set out for the new area, marching first to Locre and halting there for the midday meal. Later on, towards night, D Company proceeded to R.E. Farm, a support billet just vacated by Canadians, and stayed the night there. The Canadians left a lot of excellent ration tobacco behind them both here and in the trenches.

Next day we went forward to the new trenches. They were a change indeed from those in the Salient, and it was evident that there had not been much heavy shelling there. Instead of the high narrow trenches at Hill 60, they were mostly mere breastworks with little or no back protection. And the C.T.s were hardly deep enough to afford protection from sniping or indirect rifle fire. Fortunately the Germans did not snipe these trenches. There were three gaps in the front line, and two small posts in No Man's Land. A long winding C.T. brought you from Battalion H.Q., which were at Rossignol Farm about a mile from the front line trenches. The main features of the landscape were the Wytschaete Ridge and Petit Bois - a thick wood on our left front. The German trenches were not at first at all close to ours; and both their wire and ours was thick and solid. We had a big mine shaft in the supports, but a good way back from the front line. The Canadians told us that there had been little fighting there except between patrols and during raids. And it was evident that they had spent more time and labour in draining the trenches than in fortifying them. I had my quarters with most of the bombers in a support trench, H.5, about 250 yards from our front line. We had the trench all to ourselves and during my first visit to these trenches, which lasted six days, it was a quiet, happy home, with a green field behind and an occasional pheasant crowing in the hedges. Unfortunately for the bombers, emplacements for 60-pounder trench-mortars (worked by the R.F.A.) were already being dug at either end of our trench, and I knew there would soon be trouble for H.5. We had a curious little bombing-post outside the front line at H.4, which was only held at night. It was inside our wire, but you could only reach it by clambering over the top of the parapet after dark. The post was connected by a string to a sentry-post in the front line. And

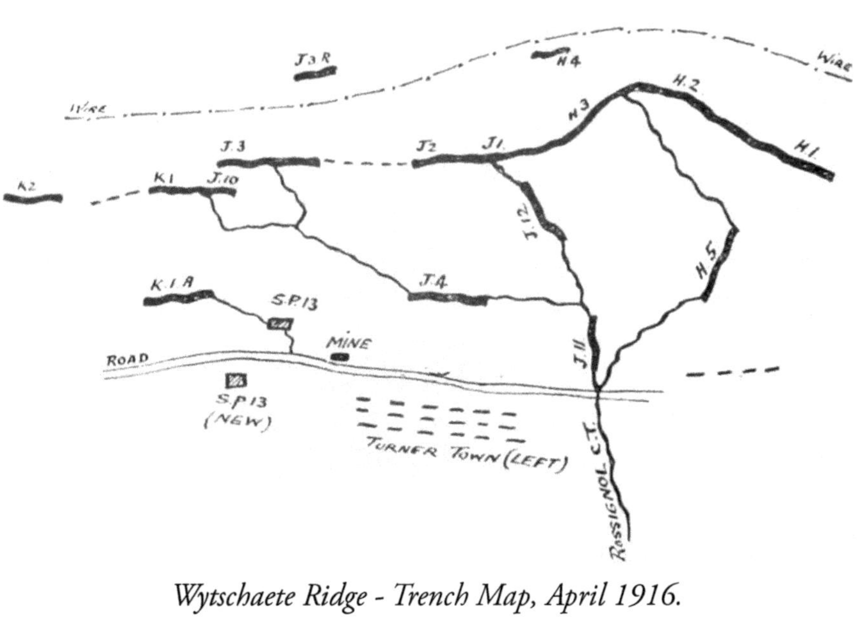

Wytschaete Ridge - Trench Map, April 1916.

various signals were arranged to warn the sentry in the front line as to what was going on, for example, two jerks on the string: 'Man returning to trench,' three jerks: 'Enemy patrol on right,' and so on. A similar bombing-post was also held at night for the first time during this visit. This was in an old broken-down trench outside our wire, called 'J.3 Right.' It was more difficult of approach owing to the mud and to its distance from the front line, and of course more dangerous because it might be attacked by the enemy's patrols. Capt. Hugh Liddell of B Company found this old trench whilst patrolling No Man's Land. It was probably once part of the front line which had become waterlogged and then abandoned. Capt. Liddell had his H.Q. in J.4 at this time. The first night he went with me to this trench with a party of bombers, and we stayed from 2 A.M. till dawn was breaking. Capt. Liddell was a great tower of strength to us in these trenches, one of the most fearless and pugnacious of men, with a taste for wandering about No Man's Land o' nights. It did you good merely to look at him.

On April 8 we were relieved by the 6th N.F., and D Company moved to a billet at R.C. Farm. One of the buildings had recently been fired by a shell, and the bodies of several horses that had been cremated inside made the air rather pungent. Whilst we were out of the line, the German artillery started shelling the trenches severely, inflicting heavy casualties on the 6th N.F., and punishing especially the support trench at J.4 and the bombers retreat at H.5. During our rest I went with Capt. Liddell and a working party of B Company to dig and fill in some cable trenches behind the supports of the 'L' Trenches. During the work I first made the acquaintance of Lieut. A.E. Odell, the Brigade Signalling Officer, who later on became a great friend. We went back to the old trenches on April 13, and I found the bombers of the 6th N.F. had moved their quarters from H.5 to Turner Town (left), two rows of small splinter-proof dugouts behind the mine shaft. The trenches were badly knocked about, and the German artillery and trench-mortars were still causing trouble. I now messed with D Company at their H.Q. in K.1.a. On the evening of April 10, I had to patrol the ground near the mine shaft with a party of bombers, to look out for a German spy who was thought to be making back this way. We saw nothing of him, but I believe that 2nd-Lieut. J. Robinson arrested a Canadian Mining Officer, who in the dark was unknown to him.

On April 18 we were relieved by the 6th N.F. their Bombing Officer, 2nd-Lieut. A. Toon, taking over from me. This time we moved back to Locre. But I was sent to B.H.Q. at Bruloose with my servant, as Lieut. W. Keene was away on leave, and it was intended that I should act for him till he came back. However I was not long at B.H.Q. before it appeared that Lieut. Keene would be returning that night. Before going off to Locre, however, I was asked to stay to dinner with the officers of B.H.Q. which I did; and it was a pleasant experience. The battalion had good quarters in Locre in the Convent School, and we soon found that a good lunch or dinner was served by the Nuns at the convent to weary officers. They also let you use the convent baths. On April 20 we held a battalion dinner there in commemoration of the Battle of St. Julien.

On Good Friday we had an Easter service, as we were to be in the trenches again on Easter Day. Our padre was Capt. Rev. J.O. Aglionby, C.F., whom we came to know and like very well. The bombers had a day's training at Bruloose, and we were asked to bring our steel helmets, which had just been issued. So I wore mine for the first time. After the practice was over, I was asked to come and see the Brigade Bombing Officer fire off some Mills rifle-grenades, which were a novelty then. Whilst this was going on a grenade burst prematurely soon after leaving the rifle, and a piece came back and struck my helmet, cutting the lining and scratching the metal. After that I would never part with that helmet, though newer ones were issued later on. Our last visit to the trenches was to be shorter, and we were to be relieved by the 3rd Division in three days. We set off on Saturday, April 22, and arrived in the C.T. all right, for the Germans seldom shelled the roads in this area. But when we got there we found things rather lively. A shell killed two or three men of D Company as they were approaching K.1.a; and Capt. Liddell and I had a splinter from another shell between us as we passed up Rossignol C.T. On arriving I got a message from the Adjutant saying, 'The G.O.C. orders that you use the greatest vigilance by day and by night.' The next day, Easter Day, the enemy shelled the trenches all day. Capt. G.F. Ball and I had an unpleasant experience in K.1.a, after lunch. For nearly two hours a howitzer battery shelled the place slowly and methodically, working up and down the little trench. Many times dirt and rubbish came flying into our shelter, but the only direct hit was on a minor structure which of course disappeared. Next day our cook-house was blown in and the crockery all smashed, but fortunately it was empty of men at the time. In these trenches it was difficult to get artillery retaliation, for the fighting at St. Eloi swallowed up most of the spare ammunition, and the allowance of shells for the batteries was small; so the enemy had a free hand in shelling our defences. Early on the Monday morning the enemy fired a shallow mine between his trenches and our own. It was a method of gaining ground, for the craters were fortified and turned into a trench. In this way the Germans began to approach fairly close to us at K.1 and J.3. I had to register with Newton rifle-grenades on the crater, but as we were short of cartridges it was not possible to fire at night.

On April 25 we were relieved by the 4th Battalion of the Royal Fusiliers, and I got away from the trenches with the last of the bombers about midnight. There was a big bombardment of these trenches next day, causing eighty casualties to the new-comers. My own little shelter was blown to pieces by a howitzer shell and the occupants killed. Nearly two years elapsed before I was again living in front line trenches.

CHAPTER VIII
DIVISIONAL REST

IN THE EARLY hours of April 20 the battalion reached Locre and spent the rest of the night in billets. By 8 A.M. we resumed our march, and went through Bailleul to Meteren. It was pleasant indeed to see the inside of a town again, and to get away from the area that was broken to bits. We were to be out of the line, we hoped, for at least a month, so naturally every one was feeling light-hearted. The bombers of the battalion were collected in a company about eighty strong, and they were billeted together under my charge. Our quarters were at a large French farm, called on the map 'Fever Farm,' and near to it was a fine set of bombing trenches. Lieut. W. Keene was also living at this farm, in order to be near the bombing ground. And we had our little mess together in the farm parlour, and our bedroom in a nice dry attic. No bombing work was done for the first three days, in order to give time for the men to get rested and to clean their equipment. The bombers were billeted in a large barn just across the yard, with plenty of clean straw inside. The French farmer and his wife were pleasant bodies, nice and friendly to us, and glad no doubt to be able to sell their light beer and eggs to the English soldier-man. The other companies of the battalion were billeted in farm-houses near Meteren. In case of an attack by the Germans on the Corps front the battalion had orders to go forward and man the trenches on Kemmel Hill. I received a paper of instructions as to what to do in case of alarm. We could tell that the Germans were causing trouble up the line, for we heard a heavy bombardment going on beyond Kemmel. About 1.30 A.M. on Sunday, April 30, the bombers' sentry came and woke me up, and I went downstairs to find a messenger had arrived with the code warning 'Kemmel Defences.' So I quickly roused the men and warned them to be ready to start in half an hour.

We hurried into our war kit and formed up in the dark outside, and soon marched off to join the rest of the battalion outside Meteren. We learned that the enemy had loosed off a lot of gas beyond Kemmel, and we were to man the defences as soon as possible. The battalion marched along as far as the entrance to Bailleul, when just as day was breaking a cyclist orderly rode up with orders for us to return to our billets. No infantry attack had followed the gas cloud, and we were free to return to rest. The Brigade had another alarm next day, but it was quickly cancelled; and after that we were not called out again. Every morning was given to bombing practice, and I offered a small prize each day for a competition in throwing. If it was wet the men stopped in the barn, and had a lecture on English or German grenades. One afternoon I walked over to Bailleul and had a bath at the Corps baths. They were rather primitive but the water was hot.

It made a nice change to get back to civilisation once more and to have a meal at a restaurant; and the shops of course were a great attraction.

About May 5, just as I was about to set out a second time for Bailleul, a letter came in for me from my brother George. It was dated the previous day and said that he was billeted with his unit close to Meteren. So I set off at once to find him, and had the good luck to meet him as he was cycling round on some medical inspection duties. His unit had just come out to France and he had no idea I was so near at hand; and I think he nearly fell off his bicycle with surprise when I first appeared in that country lane. He could not wait long then, so I asked him to come to tea with us at Fever Farm next day. And two days after that I dined with the H.Q. Mess of his unit, the 15th Hants Regiment, which I enjoyed very much. Unfortunately I saw no more of him at this time, as I left Fever Farm about May 11.

It was now decided that I should hand over the bombing to 2nd-Lieut. E.G. Lawson, a most cheery and energetic bomber, and return to company work. So I was put in command of C Company and returned with them to Locre, where I stayed for about a week. I had not much to do here, except the daily inspection of the company and orderly room. The men of the company included many of my old recruits of C

Company at Alnwick whom I was glad to see again. About May 19 I got my first leave, it was for seven clear days. And I suppose there was no happier man in France just then. The train started from Bailleul station about 6 A.M. so I had to leave Locre the night before and stay the night at an hotel at Bailleul. I had a comparatively quick journey to the coast, for we reached Boulogne at 10.45 A.M. just in time to catch the 11 o'clock boat. I arrived in Folkestone about 1.45 P.M. and in London about 3.30 P.M. the same day. Though short, it was a happy time, and I returned on May 26, staying one night in Boulogne and reaching Bailleul about midnight on Saturday, May 27. I found that the battalion was still at Locre, but the Brigade had gone back to the line, holding the same trenches on Wytschaete Ridge. An unfortunate accident had just happened in our old trenches. Lieut. W. Keene and 2nd-Lieut. Toon were both badly injured and an N.C.O. killed in the trenches by a Mills rifle-grenade, which, through a defective cartridge, fell out of the rifle and burst in the trench. So when I got back to the battalion I was told I had to proceed to B.H.Q. at Bruloose and take over the office of Brigade Bombing Officer in place of Lieut. Keene. This closed my immediate connection with the 7th N.F. for twenty months.

CHAPTER IX

BRIGADE HEAD-QUARTERS

AN INFANTRY BRIGADE Head-quarters in France could be a happy home; but only if the Brigadier was liked and respected by the rest of the Staff, and tried to make them feel at home. It seems almost an impertinence even at this date for me to say anything whether in praise or in blame of the man who controlled the immediate destinies of the 149th Infantry Brigade when I first joined it. But as I became much attached to Brigadier-General Clifford I may perhaps be forgiven for describing him rather closely. Tall and dignified, with a cold exterior and a penetrating grey eye, he had the power of commanding the respect and obedience of all. His fatalistic contempt of danger took him into the trenches wherever shelling was hottest; and it is difficult to imagine how he escaped being sniped at Hill 60 or on the Wytschaete Ridge.

He was loved by the men of the 7th N.F. as one who was willing to share their dangers, and always ready with a word of cheer in the hottest corner. 'We could have gone anywhere and done anything for him, if only he had been there to see it.' Such was the epitaph that the gallant Northumberlands gave him when he fell. I found his old-world courtesy of manner and aristocratic bearing most inspiring. And he knew the right way of getting a thing done without being cross or overbearing. A splendid type of chivalrous soldier, he stands out in my memory as a beacon of light when I have felt inclined to grumble at the Army system. I can call to mind a score of acts to me, which revealed the kindly, generous heart beneath that cold exterior. One of the first things he said to me when I joined the Brigade was this: 'Buckley, mind you make your authority felt with these adjutants. Remember, for the purposes of bombing, you are the General.' How could he have shown more generous confidence or encouraged me more for the new rôle I had to play?

Major Rowan, our Brigade-Major, was another typical officer of the old Regular Army, who was generally liked. I did not get to know him so well, as he left us for higher Staff duties before two months had passed. I always found him kind and considerate.

Capt. D. Hill had been Staff-Captain ever since the Brigade came out to France, and what he did not know about the job was not worth knowing. He often astonished me by his knowledge of what could be done, and by his serene confidence when things were looking difficult. Never ruffled, the kindest and most genial of men, he often proved a good friend and counsellor.

Capt. G.E. Wilkinson stayed with us a short time and then left to join a mess of his own Machine-Gun Officers. A man of the brightest good-humour and gaiety, he always kept us lively and amused. He went far in the war - from 2nd-Lieut. to Colonel of a battalion in eighteen months. I need say nothing further of his qualities as a soldier. He was at Oxford when I was there, and I remembered seeing him at our Law Lectures.

Lieut. G.S. Haggie, the best of fellows too, was always a kind friend to me, and made me feel at home in my new surroundings. I saw a lot of him both now and later on when we did many a strange hunt together for ammunition dumps in the most impossible of places. He was a tremendous walker and could get over really bad muddy ground at an amazing speed.

I was destined also to see much of the Brigade Signaller, Lieut. A.E. Odell, who was quite a remarkable character. He was a lion in the guise of a dove, an autocrat in the guise of a radical, a rigid disciplinarian in the guise of an army reformer. He won the M.C. and Bar and earned them both. He worked his men hard but himself harder still. He had the curious faculty of being able to work for hours by day and to spend the whole night in some muddy ditch up in the front line. His kindness to and consideration for his signallers, were only exceeded by his conscientious devotion to duty. He made me respect and like and envy him, even if he occasionally made me smile.

Major Rowan left us, I think, at La Clytte or Dranoutre, and Capt. W. Anderson became Brigade-Major in his place. He had joined the 6th N.F. at the outbreak of war and got his company and the M.C. at the Battle of St. Julien. In January 1916 he was appointed G.S.O. III at 50th Division H.Q. 'Bill' Anderson was a great man, and combined the fearlessness of the Northumbrian with a great brain. He was probably the best 'civilian' tactician in the Army, and had he decided to join the Regular Army I should have expected him to rise very high indeed. I know what the 149th Infantry Brigade owed to him; but I doubt whether many others know quite as well. And I have always thought that he was never given full scope for exercising his wonderful ability. A tall soldierly figure, with noble features and piercing blue eyes that could harden almost to ruthlessness, I carry him in my mind as my ideal of a Staff Officer. He could get men to do anything for him; his kindly tact and sympathy, his rare appreciation of your efforts, however clumsy, made you ready to work for him like a slave. He has been a good friend to me throughout, and he has done more for me than any other man in France.

At Bruloose the officers of the Brigade had small wooden huts of the Armstrong type for offices and sleeping rooms. The mess room was in the farm-house. Naturally it was a great change from the rude accommodation of a Company Mess. M. Bunge, the French interpreter, looked after our comforts well.

Next to B.H.Q. was a large and fairly useful bombing ground, where the Brigade Bombing School was carried on; and I spent a good deal of time there, as I was in charge of the school. On two days out of every four I spent the morning there, and in the afternoon I was free to visit the trenches, some four miles away. On the other two days I could go up to the trenches in the morning.

I did not miss a day's visit to the trenches and once or twice I went up twice in the day.

The journey was done on foot, so I had quite a good day's exercise. My duties in the trenches were to see that the battalions in the line had a proper supply of grenades; these were taken up by the battalion transport at night. Also that the grenades in the trenches and all bomb stores were properly stored and cleaned. I had also to see that sufficient rifle-grenades were fired at night to harass the enemy's working-parties, and that our bombing-posts were properly manned.

During our stay at Bruloose I had nearly 2000 grenades taken out of the trenches and replaced by new ones; this was hard work for the transport. But the transport officers[5] were very obliging; and I found on firing these old grenades at the school that about 30 to 40 per cent did not burst properly or even at all. The situation in the trenches was getting very bad. Shelling by the enemy's artillery was now less frequent, but the annoyance from enemy trench-mortars was something cruel. Not only large oil-cans, full of explosives, came over both by day and by night, but a horrible 9-inch trench-mortar now made its appearance and blew large craters in the C.T.s and supports. I had two of the oil-cans pretty close to me at different times, and they were not pleasant. Eventually the trench-mortaring got so severe, that the V Corps had a 12-inch howitzer brought up on the railway, and several of these huge shells were fired into Petit Bois when the German trench-mortars started. Another feature to be reckoned with was the approach of the enemy towards K.1 and J.3 by means of a series of fortified mine craters. These craters were worked on at night, and by the General's orders they had to be kept under constant fire from rifle-grenades. Several nights I went up to the trenches to see this carried out, once accompanied by the General himself. I had at the Bruloose bomb store a fairly good stock of smoke and incendiary bombs, like large cocoa tins, only containing red or white phosphorus. It occurred to me that they might be used with effect against the Germans working in the craters. So I carried a number of these bombs up to the trenches, and they were duly fired from the

5. Brigade Transport, Capt. Kinsella; 7th N.F., Capt. B. Neville; 6th N.F., Lieut. F. Clayton; 5th N.F., Lieut. M.G. Pape; 4th N.F., Lieut. W.M. Turner.

West spring-thrower or from the trench-catapult. The Germans did not seem to like them, as their discharge always drew a lot of machine-gun fire in reply. We also tried to get some more noxious bombs (e.g. 'M.S.K.'), but no supply could be obtained from the Base. The Bombing Officers[6] of the 6th and 7th N.F. carried on the harassing fire with such effect that eventually the Germans took to sending showers of 'fishtails' whenever a rifle-grenade was loosed off. The 'fishtail' was a small trench-mortar bomb, which the Germans substituted for the rifle-grenade and used with great effect. Needless to say our demonstrations were not very popular with the infantry in the front line. But Capt. Vernon Merivale, M.C., appeared to take a special delight in these harassing shoots.

6. 2nd-Lieuts. Toon and Thompson (6th N.F.) and Lawson and Woods (7th N.F.).

CHAPTER X

THE BRIGADE BOMBING SCHOOL

THE STAFF OF instructors at the Bombing School consisted of three highly trained sergeants - two of these had been instructors at the 50th Divisional Bombing School which was now given up. Sergt. Hogg of the 5th N.F. and Sergt. P. Flannigan of the 4th. N.F. took it in turns to be at the school and at the Brigade Bomb Store. So with Sergt. Moffat, who was now appointed Brigade Bombing Sergeant, I had always two to help me at the school.

On the two bombing days sixteen untrained men came from the battalion resting at Locre and sixteen others from the battalion resting at R.C. Farm.

During the two days these men had to be sufficiently instructed to throw three live Mills grenades. Generally they threw one live grenade apiece after the first day's instruction, and the two others the second day. The first thing was to give a lecture to the men, explaining the nature of the Mills grenade and the proper way to hold it and throw it.

After this a party of sixteen men were lined up in two lines, about forty yards apart, and each of the eight men in turn threw a dummy grenade towards the man opposite him. The instructor had to be careful that the man threw in the correct way and held his grenade right. The action of throwing the grenade was more like bowling overhand than throwing. After about an hour of this the first party of men, eight in number, went down to the firing-trench, which had to be 200 yards clear of any troops. There were two sandbag walls, breastworks, about five feet high - the one in front with a small traverse wall. At the front wall stood the recruit, the sergeant-instructor, and the Brigade Bombing

Officer. In front about thirty yards away was a deep pit, mostly full of water, which had been excavated by innumerable grenades thrown into it. The other seven men took refuge behind the second wall, until it was their turn to throw. Before the grenade was thrown the officer had to blow two blasts on his whistle. The first meant 'Get ready to fire' - i.e. draw the safety-pin, the second meant 'Fire.' Some men of course were more confident than others; but on the whole the Northumberlands were easy to teach, for many were miners and accustomed to explosives - in fact, it was sometimes difficult to make them take cover properly. When the grenade was thrown, every one ducked down behind the wall and waited for the explosion. If it went off all right, all was well; and the next man came along for his turn. If, however, the grenade did not go off, it had if possible to be retrieved and the detonator taken out. This was the most exciting work I had to do. Generally the sergeant and I took it in turns to pick up these 'dud' grenades as they were called. After some experience it was possible to tell the moment the grenade was thrown why it did not go off, for example the fuse might be damp and never light; or the cap might misfire; or, worst of all 'duds,' the striker might stick fast through rust or dirt.

Before I gained the experience of picking up these 'duds' and drawing their teeth, I had one lucky escape. The grenade in question had a 'hanging striker' and burst on the ground within five yards of me. It was not, I think, a very good explosion, but one of the pieces caught me on the thigh - happily it cut into the seam of my breeches and then turned, following the seam out and leaving me with a bruise and two holes in my clothes. I never liked picking up these 'duds,' but later on I got to know from the sound what was the matter with them; and then it was just a matter of experience getting them to pieces safely. The live grenades when they burst in the pit, sometimes threw out old 'dud' grenades lying in the mud. One of these latter burst in mid-air, but hurt no one; and another time the grenade dropped right into the firing-trench but did not go off. Another nasty thing was when the grenade burst too quickly; many men have been killed by premature bursts during practice. But though some grenades went off too quickly, I never had one burst in less than a second, by which time the grenade was fairly well away from the trench. Besides these thirty-two untrained men, the bombers from the battalion at Locre used to come and practise on the ground under their own Bombing Officer. But if any of these men wished to pass the live firing test, to qualify them to wear the Bombers badge (a red grenade on the right arm), I had to test them with six live grenades. Three out of the six had to fall within a narrow trench about twenty-five yards from the firing point.

Of course I had to watch the grenade till it reached the ground - and pray that it would not burst prematurely. What a blessing those steel helmets were during live bombing practice! They were proof against bomb splinters and gave you a feeling of confidence.

The battalion bombers were also trained at the school to fire live rifle-grenades. No risks were taken with the Newton rifle-grenade; during firing all men had to be behind a barricade and the rifle was fired off with a string and held in position by an iron stand. But we used to think the Hales rifle-grenade quite safe, so that men were trained to fire off these grenades holding the rifle to the ground in the kneeling position. On one occasion several of us had a lucky escape. The grenade burst at the end of the rifle, instead of bursting 120 yards away on contact with the ground. Sergt. Hogg and another bomber of the 5th N.F. were holding the rifle and both got knocked over, Sergt. Hogg with a slight cut on the head, the latter shaken but unhurt. The Bombing Officer of the 5th N.F. and I both got scratched on the face with splinters.

During our stay at Bruloose about 420 men went through the recruits' course and over 1700 grenades were fired.

Later on I had to be content with much less elaborate bombing grounds. Sometimes they had to be improvised from nothing, at other times a bombing-pit of a sort was found, and we had to make the best of it. After the battle on the Somme far less attention was paid to bombing; but for a time it was thought desirable to have every man trained in bombing, even at the expense of the rifle.

CHAPTER XI

ST. ELOI AND NEUVE EGLISE

ABOUT JULY 2 the Brigade came out of the line for a short time, and B.H.Q. moved to a camp between Mont Rouge and Westoutre. During this stay I was able to carry on the training at the Bruloose Bombing School. There was a fine view of the trenches from Mont Rouge. We could of course hear the sound of the bombardment on the Somme, but at this distance it was more distinct some days than others.

On July 14 the Brigade went into the line again, south of St. Eloi, the support trenches being in Ridge Wood. B.H.Q. moved to a camp at La Clytte, farther than ever from the front line trenches.

At La Clytte there was a small bombing ground, but it was not very safe for live practice, and I was glad when we left it. We did not stay long in these trenches; but before we left them the bombers of the 6th N.F. killed a German and he was brought back to our trenches. It was the first dead German that I had seen.

Our next move was to a quieter part of the line, namely to Wulverghem, below the Messines Ridge. B.H.Q. went to a canvas camp at Neuve Eglise, but moved soon after to Dranoutre, where we were billeted in houses. Lieut.-Col. Turner, O.C. the 5th N.F., came to command the Brigade for about a week, in the absence of General Clifford, who went to England on leave. He was a regular officer, with a keen sense of humour and with an extraordinary dislike of parsons. These new trenches were quiet enough, but the sniping of the enemy was far too good. I was nearly caught out before I realised that fact. I was looking over the parapet the first day with L.-C. Austin, when a bullet caught the edge of the parapet just in front of us, tearing the sandbag along the top and stopping within a few inches of our heads. Of course we dropped down quickly into the trench, but L.-C. Austin waved his cap over the top to signal a 'miss.' He told me it would never do to let the German sniper think he had scored a hit. The 'flying pig,' our large trench-mortar, was first used in a bombardment of the German trenches here, and I believe our Stokes mortar battery did a record rate of fire on the same occasion. We had a lot of gas cylinders stored in the front line trenches ready for use. But they were not required and we had the pleasant job of removing them. They were always talked about as 'rum jars.'

There was no bombing ground at Dranoutre, and I had to make a place for live practice in a farmer's field, much to his disgust. 'C'est la guerre, monsieur!' was all we could say to his expostulations. We could now hear the great cannonade on the Somme going on to the south almost day and night.

A large number of wooden ammunition huts were erected along the roads near Dranoutre, and heavy gun emplacements were being made about Kemmel. Perhaps it was intended that the Fifth Army should make a big push here, if the battle on the Somme had been more successful at the start.

About August 7 we were relieved by two shattered divisions from the Somme, one of them being the Ulster Division that had seen hard fighting south of Serre. We had a good idea whither we were bound. But at first we moved off to the Meteren area, where B.H.Q. were quartered in a camp of wooden huts for about five days. The censorship now became very strict, no inkling of our movements was to be given to anyone at home. Valises too had to be lightened by sending home all spare kit; and all papers and maps relating to the Kemmel area had to be destroyed or returned. Amongst other things I sent home my 'slacks,' and never wore them again in France. About August 11 we moved off to Bailleul railway station and entrained there, leaving about midnight. Next morning we reached Doullens, where we left the train. The R.T.O. at Doullens was Capt. Rearden, whom I knew as a boy at Wellington

College and had not seen for sixteen years. But he recognised me and claimed acquaintance.

We marched that day to Fienvillers, and stayed there two days in a French house. The next move was to Naours where we spent one night; and the next night we stayed at Pierregot. On August 17 we marched to the wood at Hénencourt.

The whole Brigade was encamped in the neighbourhood of the wood. We had at last arrived in the rest area of the Somme front, and it could only be a matter of days before we were involved in the great battle. But before that could happen there was a great deal to do to prepare the men for their ordeal, and perhaps not a great deal of time in which to do it. The Division was served out with the short rifle for the first time. Hitherto we had only had the long rifle such as was used in the South African War.

CHAPTER XII

THE SOMME[7]

THE BATTLE ON the Somme was to me the great tragedy of the war. A glorious noble tragedy, but still a tragedy. Both sides of course have claimed the victory, the British a tactical one, the Germans a strategic one. The net result to the Allies from a material point of view was the recapture of some hundreds of square miles of France, for the most part battered to bits and as desolate and useless as a wilderness; and the capture or destruction of so many thousands of the enemy at a cost altogether out of proportion to their numbers. The Germans claim, and claim quite rightly, that they frustrated our attempt to break through their line. On the other hand it can be little consolation for them to know that a nation of amateur soldiers[8] drove them out of the strongest fortress in the world; drove them out so completely that they were glad to take refuge, morally as well as physically, behind their famous Hindenburg Line.

No doubt our grand attack lasting from July to November 1916 cemented the Alliance with France and saved Verdun from falling. No doubt it paved the way, in knowledge and morale, for further attacks at a later date. The fact remains that before its lessons were learnt the slopes of the Ancre and the Somme were sown with the bodies of thousands of the finest specimens of the British race. What a cost was paid for the example and the lesson! Never again during the war had Britain such fine athletic men, such gallant and heroic sons to fight her battles. No horror or hardship could subdue their spirit. Again and again, through shattered ranks and over ground covered with the fallen, they went

7. See Illustration, p. 67.
8. I allude of course to the New Armies.

forward to the supreme sacrifice as cheerfully and as light-heartedly as if they were out for a holiday. They knew they could beat the enemy in front of them, and they went on and did it again and again, in spite of the wire, in spite of the mud, in spite of thousands of machine-gun bullets and shells. The tragedy of it all is written in one word. *Waste* - waste of lives, waste of effort, waste of ammunition. The fact is now clear that in 1916 the resources of the British Nation were not sufficiently developed to smash the German war machine. That was undoubtedly the hope of every one who took part in the battle, to deliver a final knock-out blow. But this hope failed, even if it failed by a little. Our artillery, mighty as it undoubtedly was, was not mighty enough yet to destroy the enemy's defences and to shatter his power of resistance. Alas, it was a blow that could never be repeated again with such magnificent human resources!

After the supreme effort by all ranks a terrible wave of depression naturally followed. And can this be wondered at? For a time there was lack of confidence which made itself all too apparent in 1917, a year of unparalleled disasters. No one who has not set out with such high hopes can know how awful that depression can be.

The effort of the British Army was never so united, never so intense as it was in the battle on the Somme. Later on reverses brought knowledge and knowledge at last brought victory. But for some that victory had its sad side too; for thousands upon thousands of those gay and gallant comrades in the Great Endeavour were not there to share it.[9]

The part of the 50th Division in the battle was not a small one. Briefly the Division went into the Somme area on August 17, 1916, and left it about March 10, 1917. Their first attack was launched on September 15, 1916, in company with the Guards and some of the finest divisions in the British Army. After almost continuous fighting they were withdrawn about October 5, and went back to the rest area around Hénencourt till October 21 - after having advanced their line from High Wood Ridge to the edge of Le Sars.

---

9. These views of the battle, I am told, are unduly pessimistic. But I let them stand as a record of personal feelings aroused as a result of the battle.

On October 25 they returned to the same front and made two gallant but fruitless attacks on the Butte of Warlencourt, in support of larger operations about Beaumont Hamel. The hardship of the fighting between October 25 and November 16 cannot be realised by those who did not actually experience the conditions. From December 28 to January 23 the Division held the line south of Le Barque and Ligny-Thilloy. After that they moved farther south and held the line in front of Belloy and Estrées, trenches that had been captured by the French. No wonder, after this hard work, that the 50th Division gained the reputation of a hard fighting division.

I can give no very accurate idea of the casualties suffered by the Division; but some idea of the losses may be drawn from the casualties among the bombers of the 7th N.F. Of these I have fairly accurate details. The bombers of the 7th N.F. went into action on September 15, 1916, about eighty strong - ten N.C.O.s and seventy men. When the roll was called at Bresle on November 20, 1916, eleven men alone answered. Of the N.C.O.'s two were wounded and the rest were killed. The bombers of the 4th N.F. suffered almost as heavily, but I have now no details.

CHAPTER XIII
HÉNENCOURT

BRIGADE HEAD-QUARTERS WERE accommodated in wooden huts, but the battalions were mostly under canvas. Strenuous efforts had now to be made to complete the training of the men, and to initiate them to a style of warfare that was quite new and strange to them.

My own task was to train as many men as possible in the use of the Mills grenade. Each day I had fifty men to train, and they were kept at it all morning and again in the evening, until they had each thrown two live grenades. I had the services of three sergeant-instructors, who were invaluable in getting the men past the first stage. All the live firing I had to supervise myself; that being the rule of the Army, that an officer should always be present during live practice. All my spare time was spent in going over and testing the grenades to be fired next day, or in baling out the bombing trench, which filled very rapidly in wet weather. And so it went on day after day. Thirteen officers and 671 men who had never previously thrown a live grenade went through the course at Hénencourt; and about 1400 live grenades were fired. The battalion bombers used the ground in the afternoon in charge of their own officers; and they got through another 1000 grenades. On September 2 I was able to tell the General that every man in the Brigade, including machine-gunners and trench-mortar men, had been through the course, with which he expressed himself very pleased. Towards the end of our stay the General came to see the live throwing several times in the evenings, and he always spoke very encouragingly to the men.

About September 6 I went with a party of officers from the Brigade to view the trenches we were to take over on the Somme battlefield. And as this was my first visit there it naturally made a great impression on me. We started off in the dark and rode through Hénencourt and Millencourt to Albert. Just before we reached Albert we passed through a cloud of lachrymatory gas, which made me weep copious tears for nearly half an hour. The great sight in Albert was of course the ruined cathedral, with its colossal statue of the Virgin and Child hanging downwards over the roadway. We rode on to where the front line had been at Fricourt then to Fricourt 'Circus,' Mametz, and then to the south of Mametz Wood, where we left our horses. First we went through the wood to B.H.Q., which were in some deep dugouts there. Having obtained guides and a rough sort of map, we went on to Battalion H.Q. at the Chalk Quarry east of Bazentin-le-Petit. This was about 1000 yards from the front line, which lay just below the ridge from Martinpuich to High Wood. A deep C.T. called 'Jutland Alley' took us up to the front line - 'Clark's Trench.' So far we had little trouble from shelling, but we passed over the bodies of two unfortunate Highlanders in Jutland Alley who had been recently killed by a shell. The entrance to Intermediate Trench on the left was terrible, the smell being overpowering. As a matter of fact there were scores of dead men just out of sight on both sides of this trench, whom it had been impossible to bury. It was not unusual to see an arm or leg protruding out of the side of the C.T., so hastily had the Germans buried their dead. And there were swarms and swarms of flies everywhere. When we had finished looking round in the front line, which was a good trench and quite quiet, we turned back down Jutland Alley. The German 'heavies' were now shelling the supports and close to the C.T. One shell, which seemed not to explode, hit the edge of the C.T.; and when we got to the place we found the trench partially filled in and an unfortunate man buried up to his neck, much shaken but not much hurt. We left him to be extricated by his friends who had got spades. I then visited the trenches near the windmill and then returned to the south of Mametz Wood. Whilst waiting here I examined with interest the many curious little 'cubby holes' that our troops had made during the attack on Mametz Wood. I also watched the German 'heavies' shelling our field batteries near Bazentin-le-Grand, and sending up clouds of chalky dust. A few shrapnel shells were also fired near the road, and I believe our horses and orderlies were nearly hit, but escaped by galloping off when the first shell came. The countryside looked very desolate and knocked about till we got to Fricourt Circus, only the chalky roads were crammed with limbers and lorries taking up supplies. At the Circus there was a remarkable sight, a huge camping ground covering several square miles, every available spot on it packed with dumps and horse-lines, artillery parks, bivouacs, and tents. All the roads round here were full of troops on the move, and of lines and lines of lorries either coming or going. After passing Albert there was less of interest, but we saw one of our aeroplanes stranded in a ploughed field east of Millencourt. The pilot told us he had got his machine damaged over the German line, but had managed to get back thus far, when he had made a bad landing. Such was my first visit to the great battlefield, a dreary looking spot with a general aspect of chalk, broken stumps of trees, and crowded muddy roads.

Our stay at Hénencourt was drawing to a close, but before we left we had an inspection by the III Corps Commander. And on the last day, September 9, we held a grand sports day and had a band playing. The men looked splendidly fit and well after their month's rest, and they displayed a wonderful spirit, talking eagerly of their part in the coming attack. Alas and alas! At times I could have wept to see these splendid bronzed men go marching by, the very flower of our English race. For I knew that very soon I should see few of them again, or few indeed of their like.

CHAPTER XIV
MAMETZ WOOD

ON SUNDAY SEPTEMBER 10, the Brigade left Hénencourt, and B.H.Q. went to the deep dugouts in Mametz Wood. I travelled there with Sergts. Moffat and Hogg, and we were lucky enough to get good lifts, first in a Canadian Staff car and then on a motor-lorry. Capt. Bloomer (5th D.L.I. and attached to B.H.Q.) shared a deep dugout with me, and we had meals together.

It was the first deep dugout I had entered, and of course it was the work of the Germans. There were about twenty steps down at either end, the wooden sides of the stairway scarred with bullet holes and splinters. Inside there were just two narrow apartments, one for our bedroom and the other for meals. Though rather draughty it was comfortable enough and practically shell-proof. Capt. Bloomer had an unpleasant job, which kept him out late at nights, and I did not envy him. In order to make the attack, it was decided to dig a forward trench some way in front of Clark's Trench. The digging was done at night and cost us a number of casualties from shell and rifle fire. Capt. Bloomer used to go up every night to see the work done.

The second morning at Mametz Wood I was greatly shocked to hear that our Brigadier had been killed by a sniper from High Wood, as he was going out to inspect the forward trench just after dawn. It was nearly two days before his body could be brought in, owing to the shelling that went on at night. He was buried at Albert. A few days later Brigadier-General Ovens, an Irishman, came to take command of the 149th Infantry Brigade.

My job was now to prepare the Brigade bomb stores and to see that the grenades were properly packed into sandbag carriers for taking up the line. A special dugout had been prepared as a bomb store near the

Chalk Quarry at Bazentin-le-Petit, but almost at the last moment the R.A.M.C. commandeered the place for their forward dressing-station. So the boxes of grenades had to lie in the open in large shell-holes, covered with German greatcoats, mackintosh sheets, or anything else we could get hold of. I spent hours and hours examining the grenades and packing them into sandbag carriers. One of our transport-wagons[10] had a lucky escape, whilst carrying a load of 2000 Mills grenades, all detonated, to one of our dumps. The safety-pin of one of the grenades broke with the jolting of the wagon, and the grenade went off, bursting its own and several other boxes, but not setting off any other of the grenades. I had an anxious time unpacking that wagon-load. The brass safety-pins of the Mills grenades were very unsatisfactory at this time; but I had collected a large number of steel pins from the bombing grounds, and I used to re-pin any that I thought had weak brass-pins. This examination of the grenades was rather wearisome, but it was time well spent, for we had no accident with them when the carrying-parties took them up the line. And other units were not so fortunate in that respect. About 24,000 grenades went through my hands, and of these perhaps 5000 went into the sandbags. On September 14 we first saw the mysterious tanks, which had arrived behind the quarry to take part in the great attack next day. We had two allotted to our Division. That night we moved from Mametz Wood to the Chalk Quarry at Bazentin-le-Petit. Here one of the Divisional Field Co. R.E. had prepared for us excellent H.Q. in the side of the Quarry. The offices were well down in the side of the Quarry, the mess room was a large shelter covered with sandbags a little higher up. We were fairly crowded that night, for a large number of 'liaison' officers arrived for duty next day. We were sleeping inside the mess shelter, practically shoulder to shoulder all over the floor. Officers were sleeping and feeding and working there all at the same time. A day and night mess was run for the benefit of all that came in.

For the last four or five days our artillery had kept up an almost continual fire on the enemy's lines. Now at the last moment the guns

10. Lieut. F.C. Clayton was now Brigade Transport Officer.

of the Field Artillery were taken out of their hiding places and brought forward into the open. Our chalk pit was practically under the muzzles of about a dozen field guns.

Later on that night we heard a curious whistling, puffing sound, it was the two tanks clambering up the hill to get into position near the front line.

CHAPTER XV

THE 15TH SEPTEMBER 1916

WE WERE ALL up early next morning, and got some breakfast well before dawn. The air outside had a regular autumn chill. At first only an occasional gun fired in the distance. But about twenty minutes before dawn, our heavy guns opened their bombardment. To one standing in the quarry, below the level of the ground, they had the most weird of sounds. A dull rumbling in the rear and a continual whizz and hiss high overhead. Hardly a sound of the guns firing and no sound of the shells bursting. Only that terrible grinding swish in the air above. Twenty minutes of that, and then, with a terrific roar, all our field guns opened, and we knew that our comrades in front, the 4th N.F. on the right and the 7th N.F. on the left, had 'gone over the top.' The noise in front of the field batteries was pandemonium, excruciating to the nerves. The air shook and quivered with the sound, the quarry seemed to shake. You could only hear when the speaker shouted in your ear. And so it went on hour by hour all day. The rate of fire subsided, but the guns went on all day. I was standing with the Staff-Captain in the Quarry, when I got what felt like a stone in the face. It proved to be a piece of a shell, but happily for me it struck the ground first and caught me on the rebound. A small cut about the nose and chin, but I had to go and have it dressed. I got well chaffed afterwards on my rather comical appearance. It was an anxious time before the first news got back, but when it did it was good. Our men had taken the first German trench, and were waiting to go ahead again. Unfortunately High Wood was not taken by the 47th Division on our right till midday, and meanwhile we lost numerous casualties from having our right flank exposed to

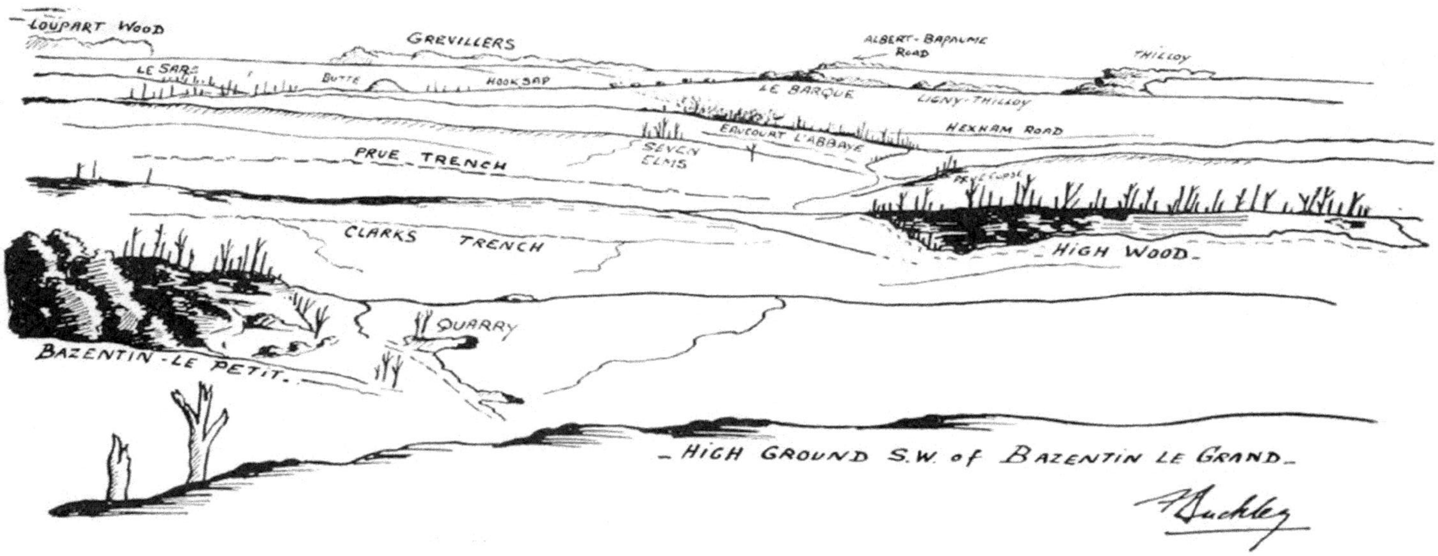

Scene of Attacks by 50th Division. Sept. 15-Nov. 14, 1916.

machine-gun fire. A report came in that a large party of Germans were starting a bombing attack on our right, so it was decided to send up a supply of grenades. I went, therefore, and found Lieut. Mackenzie, who was in charge of 100 men acting as carriers, and handed over 2400 grenades. This party went up to the front line and back without mishap. But shortly afterwards Lieut. Mackenzie was badly wounded by one of our own shells bursting prematurely. We had fifty casualties at the Quarry from premature bursts. It was not the fault of the gunners, but either the guns were worn or the shells were defective.

I lost two sergeant-instructors in the Quarry. Sergt. Moffat was badly hit in the thigh with a fragment from a premature and died a few days after. Sergt. Hogg was wounded in the chest by a bullet, but not fatally. The wounded and prisoners began to stream back past the Quarry. And as they came we began to get news of our friends in front. Though successful the Brigade had to pay a heavy price. The 4th N.F. were literally cut to pieces. I lost many friends killed, including Capt. J.W. Merivale, 2nd-Lieut. J. Robinson, and Sergt. Austin, and many more wounded, including Capt. G.F. Ball.[11] During the attack thirty-seven out of the eighty bombers of the 7th N.F. were killed or wounded, and the bombers of the 4th N.F. paid a still heavier price, including their gallant officer killed.

At 4 P.M. the 151st Infantry Brigade took over the operations on our front and continued the attack at night. Next day B.H.Q. returned to Mametz Wood.[12] I had to pay a visit to the nearest large dressing-station to get the anti-tetanus inoculation. This proved more troublesome than the small cut I received, and it made me feel fairly weak for the next ten days. On September 20 I went with Capt. D. Hill to select a place for a dump near High Wood, and we passed over the first captured German trench. There were few of our men lying about, for the burial parties

11. The two other Company Commanders of the 7th N.F., Capt. V. Merivale, M.C., and Capt. E.F. Clennell, M.C., got safely through the action.

12. At this place I first had the opportunity of speaking to our Divisional Commander, Major-General Sir P.S. Wilkinson, K.C.M.G., C.B., who was beloved by every one in the Division.

had been hard at work. But farther back around Intermediate Trench there were piles of British and German soldiers still lying where they had fallen weeks before. We had now to get a number of sandbag carriers made for taking more grenades up the line, and I was given a small party from the 5th N.F. to get this done.

About September 22 we returned to the line, and B.H.Q. to the Chalk Quarry at Bazentin-le-Petit. I have but a confused recollection of the period from now to the end of our stay in this locality. My servant had a lucky escape in the Quarry. He was sitting outside my dugout with two others making some tea, when a small shell fell right in the middle of their feet. All were thrown over by the explosion, but only one was really hurt - Capt. Bloomer's servant. We brought the poor fellow into the dugout, with his right arm almost severed at the elbow; and we spent the next ten minutes tying him up as best we could. He died about a week later. I also remember paying two visits to a most unpleasant spot selected as the Brigade ammunition dump, at the junction of Crescent Alley and Spence Trench. The German artillery never seemed to leave it alone.

About October 3 the 5th N.F., commanded by Lieut.-Col. N.I. Wright attacked the Flers Line, and took two trenches. Before this attack started a huge howitzer was brought up and placed on the west side of Mametz Wood. And during the one and a half hours preceding the attack, it fired sixty 15-inch shells into Le Sars, of which only two failed to burst. On October 5 the 50th Division was relieved, and B.H.Q. moved back to a doctor's house in Albert. That night General Ovens gave a dinner to the officers of the Staff at a restaurant in the town, where a good repast was served by some French civilians. Next day we moved farther back to Millencourt, and we were billeted in a nice house.

CHAPTER XVI

MILLENCOURT

I WENT OFF to Millencourt, on October 6, in front of the rest of Brigade in order to look for a bombing ground. I found one all right, but I cannot say that it was altogether safe or in very good condition. The firing-trench was a square emplacement cut into the ground and there was no easy exit in case of trouble; also our predecessors there obviously had had an accident on the spot, for I found a box of Mills grenades lying there, half buried, two or three of the grenades exploded and the rest more or less damaged and in a dangerous condition. However, the mess was cleared up at last, and I had to make the best of the place, such as it was. I had now only Sergt. P. Flannigan to help me, but Lieut.-Col. Scott Jackson, D.S.O., my colonel, kindly allowed L.-Sergt. Piercy of the 7th N.F. to come and assist in the training at the Brigade Bombing School. After the heavy fighting the Brigade was supplied with large drafts of new men. They came chiefly from the Fen country and were only partially trained. I found them far more difficult to instruct in bombing than the Northumberland miners. I had between forty and fifty of these men each day, and they had to throw two live grenades before they left. One exciting event happened during this training. One of the drafts was about to throw his grenade, when he dropped it and of course it started to burn. With great quickness and resolution Sergt. Flannigan picked it up and got it out of the trench before it burst - and his action undoubtedly averted a tragedy. Many men have received decorations for similar acts in the trenches, but the Brigade decided that nothing could be done in this case except mentioning it in Divisional Orders and recording it in the Sergeant's pay book. After this I arranged with the Sergeant to keep an undetonated grenade handy, and if any man seemed too nervous to throw his first grenade safely, we supplied him with this. He went through all the emotions of throwing a live grenade, and endangered neither himself nor us. The empty grenade was then picked up and treated as a 'dud,' i.e. one that had misfired. Between October 7 and October 21, 477 new men went through the bombing course, and nearly a thousand grenades were fired. Shortly after this Sergt. P. Flannigan went to the Corps School, first as a bomber and afterwards as a Lewis gun instructor; and I never had his services again.

Brigadier-General Ovens was a pleasant, genial Irishman, who tried to make us all feel at home in his mess. But I doubt whether the Irish really understand the Northumbrians or vice versa. At this time John Coates, the famous tenor singer, came out as a lieutenant in the Yorkshire Regiment. He was attached to us for a time. It was a sporting thing for him to do, but he was neither young enough nor hard enough to stand the severities of the campaign. He acted as General's Orderly-Officer for a time and afterwards became Town Major of Bécourt, not an easy or a very pleasant job. He sang several times for the men, once in the open air, and his singing was certainly top hole.

During this stay at Millencourt I paid a flying visit to Amiens with Lieut. A.E. Odell. We went there and back in a Divisional Signal car and stopped only a few hours, in fact for dinner.

About October 24 we went to Albert, stopping one night at the same house as before, and next day we went back to the line.

CHAPTER XVII
HOOK SAP

ON OCTOBER 25, 1916, we took over from a brigade of the 1st Division at the ruined sugar factory at Bazentin-le-Grand. The sleeping apartments were in a dugout below ground, but the mess room and offices were in the building on the ground floor. After arriving I went with a bombing sergeant of the Black Watch to have a look at the Brigade Dump, which was a good way from B.H.Q. You got at it by walking across country to the west end of High Wood, and then along a trench tramway till it ended rather abruptly at the Flers Switch. Like most dumps, it was at the end of the tramway and none too healthy a spot. It was afterwards moved forward to a sunken road called 'Hexham Road,' where the boxes of ammunition were just piled in the open.

The position in front was now as follows. The 1st Division had pushed the enemy back to a line along the top of a ridge running from the Butte of Warlencourt practically due east. This ridge prevented our seeing the enemy's approaches and support positions in Le Barque. On the other hand from Loupart Wood the whole of our approaches and support trenches were in full view of the enemy, as far back as High Wood. Across those two miles no one could move in daylight without being seen by the enemy, and there was practically no position to put our field guns forward of High Wood. The enemy's front line consisted of two trenches - Gird Line and Gird Support - with a forward trench on the top of the ridge, called on the left 'Butte Trench' on the right 'Hook Sap.' Our front line Snag Trench and Maxwell Trench lay this side the ridge and about two hundred yards away from the German forward trench.

The Butte of Warlencourt, an old Gallic burial place, was a round chalk hill, rising about 100 feet above ground level; and had been mined with deep dugouts and made into a formidable strong point. From the Butte machine-guns defended the approaches to Hook Sap, and from Hook Sap and the Gird Line machine-guns defended the approaches to the Butte. The ground between and around the opposing trenches had been ploughed up with innumerable shells, some of huge calibre, and it was now a spongy morass, difficult to cross at a walk and impossible at a run. As events proved, unless both the Butte and the Gird Line could be taken at the same time, the one would render the other impossible to hold. This then was the problem that faced the 50th Division, a problem that would have been difficult enough in the driest of weather, but rendered four times more so by the rain which fell in deluges on three days out of four during the whole of October and November. I have dealt with these details rather fully, because this phase of the Somme battle has been passed over as a thing of no account. The eyes of the public have been directed to the successful operations at Beaumont Hamel and Beaucourt. They have not been directed to the misery and horror that were endured heroically but unavailingly on the slopes between Eaucourt L'Abbaye and Le Barque. Never have the soldiers of the 50th Division deserved more and won less praise than they did during the operations between October 25 and November 15. I have no pen to describe the conditions that were faced by the brave men, who, after labouring unceasingly in the slimy horrors and rain for three weeks without rest or relief, stormed and took Hook Sap, only to be cut off and killed to the last man by successive counter-attacks. It is a sorrowful page in the history of the 7th N.F., but for stark grim courage and devotion to duty it cannot be surpassed by anything in the history of the battalion.

The first attack on the Butte and Butte Trench took place about the beginning of November and was made by the 151st Infantry Brigade. On the right the attack did not succeed; but on the left the troops reached the Butte and took or killed many Germans. Unfortunately the machine-guns behind the Butte prevented the Brigade from consolidating the ground won, and the troops eventually retired to their original line. During this operation the men of the 149th Infantry Brigade were employed in carrying up stores and as stretcher parties. Eventually, about November 12, the Brigade took over the front line, with a view to renewing the attack whenever the weather should permit. Our H.Q. were established at Seven Elms, about a mile from the front line, with rear H.Q. at the sugar factory. At dawn on November 14 the Brigade attacked the Hook Sap and Gird Line, the 5th N.F. on the right, the 7th N.F. on the left opposite the sap. At the same time an Australian Corps attacked farther to the right, but no attack was made on the Butte itself. An officer, who was in the trenches south-west of the Butte and saw the Northumberlands go forward, told me that he had never seen such a strange sight. The men staggered forward a few yards, tumbled into shell-holes or stopped to pull out less fortunate comrades, forward a few more yards, and the same again and again. All the while the machine-guns from the German trenches poured a pitiless hail into the slowly advancing line; and the German guns opened out a heavy barrage on the trenches and on the ground outside. In spite of mud, in spite of heavy casualties, the survivors of two companies of the 7th N.F. struggled across that spongy swamp and gained the German line. What happened after that can only be conjectured, for they never kept touch with the 5th N.F., who reached and took the Gird Line. But it is known that the 7th N.F. got a footing both in Hook Sap and in the Gird Line behind. The Germans barraged the captured trenches twice or three times during the day, and are thought to have attacked them in force with fresh reserves each time. Owing to the heavy and continuous barrage across No Man's Land no news could be got back and no supports could be sent forward. Finally, at night, the remnants of the shattered brigade were collected, and another attempt made to reach the trenches; but the Germans had evidently now got back to their old position and in the mud and darkness the fresh attack had little chance of success. Nothing more has been seen or heard of the two companies that reached Hook Sap. It is believed that they perished to the last man, overwhelmed by successive German counter-attacks. Second-Lieut. E.G. Lawson fell at Hook Sap, also 2nd-Lieut. R.H.F. Woods, both Bombing Officers of the 7th N.F.; also Bombing Sergts. J.R. Richardson and J. Piercy.

The 5th N.F. did well indeed, for they succeeded in holding their ground in the Gird Line and handed it over next day to the troops that relieved them. But that also had to be abandoned at last, owing to its isolated position.

The only consolation that can be drawn from this heroic but tragic affair is that it may have created a diversion to our successful operations at Beaucourt. As an isolated operation it was doomed from the start owing to the state of the ground and the exhaustion of the men who took part in it.

My own part in the sufferings of the Brigade at this time was so insignificant that it is not worth giving many details of my experiences. I found walking over the muddy ground most terribly exhausting, especially in a trench coat dripping with rain and mud. And it was a long way, over three miles, from rear H.Q. to the dump at Hexham Road. One morning I went with Major Anderson to the ruins of Eaucourt L'Abbaye on a visit of inspection. For months this was a terribly shelled place, and it was now nothing but a pile of broken sticks and brickdust. We were lucky to get clear of it before the morning hate began. There were still large numbers of British and German dead lying in heaps round the Flers Line; and two broken down tanks completed the picture of muddy desolation. On November 14, the day of the battle, I went up to advanced B.H.Q. at Seven Elms, where quarters were very crowded. I remember being so tired out that night that I fell asleep standing in one of the passages, propped against one of the walls. Next day I returned to the sugar factory. And on November 17 B.H.Q. moved back to a billet in Albert. Here, on November 19, I attended the Battalion Church Parade in a barn. A mere handful of men, gaunt, hollow-cheeked, and exhausted, their faces dead white and their clothes almost in rags, it was one of the saddest parades I can remember.

During this visit to the line I first had the services of Pte. Fairclough of the 5th N.F. as my Brigade Bombing Orderly, and he remained with me in that capacity till I left the Brigade in 1918. I found him a most useful, willing man, and he soon gained his lance stripe. On November 19, owing to the kindness of Major Anderson, I was granted leave to

England for ten days. He told the General that I was looking rather war-worn and that I should be needed for further grenade training on my return.

It was during this visit to Bazentin-le-Grand that I first started studying Intelligence work. The Brigade-Major asked me to spend my spare time in assisting him with some aeroplane photographs. I had to go over the daily series that came in from the Corps, and note anything new on our own part of the front. Major Anderson was an expert reader of these photographs, and he taught me all I know about the subject. I found it an interesting subject, and it was to have a great influence over my future career.

CHAPTER XVIII

SECOND LEAVE - BRESLE

MY JOURNEY FROM Albert to England was remarkable for the hardships that occurred. It should be remembered that every one was desperately tired and worn out already. We were told to appear at Albert station at midnight. When we got there we were told to expect the train at 2.15 A.M. This meant walking about the platform to keep warm, for there was no shelter for officers at the station. Capt. J.O. Aglionby, C.F., our padre, and Capt. Lidderdale, R.A.M.C, our battalion doctor, were both going by the same train, so I was not without company. When 2.15 A.M. came there was no train, and we kept walking about till dawn broke, but still no train. The R.T.O. then told us that there had been a breakdown and that the train could not be expected for a long time. So we decided to go and get breakfast at our billets and then to go to Amiens by motor-lorry, and catch the train there. At least there would be less chance of being shelled there, and some food and shelter.

So we set off about 10 o'clock and eventually got to Amiens, where we had a decent lunch. We had to keep hanging about the station, however, inquiring for the train. It arrived about 9 P.M., about eighteen hours late, and we were glad enough to get on board. It is difficult enough to sleep sitting in a train, but I think I managed a few hours of troubled sleep. And next morning we arrived in Le Havre. The first thing there was to march the men down to a rest camp a long way from the town, and a good way from the docks. We were told to report back at the same place at 2.30 P.M. So we trudged back to Le Havre and got shaved and fed. On returning to the Rest Camp we were told that the boat would leave in twenty minutes and that, as it was a good thirty minutes walk, we had better be quick. Fortunately we got hold of a motor-car and got a lift part of the way and hurried along after that as fast as we could. When we reached the dock we found the boat would not leave for another two hours. The organisation here was rotten just at this time, but it improved later. *The Viper*, a fast packet-boat, took us across to Southampton. And next morning I proceeded to Weston-super-Mare, having taken nearly three days on the journey. Most of that leave I spent in bed in the hands of the doctor. I was utterly worn out, not only with exhaustion, but with the depression naturally caused by losing so many friends and comrades in a manner apparently so fruitless.

The company of recruits I had at Alnwick, was practically wiped out, I found about two of them with the battalion when I returned. Only eleven were left of the battalion bombers, my good comrades of the Salient. The Bombing Officers of the four battalions were all casualties, four of them killed. There were few trained bombers left in the whole brigade. I went back to France on December 2 in anything but buoyant spirits.

On returning to Albert I found that the Brigade were billeted at the small village of Bresle. And I got there without much difficulty. The weather was wet and cold, as it generally is in December; but active preparations were soon started for getting the Bombing School open. We found a fairly good bombing-pit for the Brigade School, but we had to make one for the battalions. I was now without trained instructors and I had no Brigade Bombing Sergeant, but I was lent Corp. Munro, a bomber from the 6th N.F., and I made what use I could of Pte. Fairclough, my orderly. The result was that I had not only to attend to all the live firing, but I had to do the sergeants' work as well. Afterwards there were the grenades to be sorted out for next day and a friendly hand given to the Bombing Officers of the battalions, most of whom were new to their work.

During our stay at Bresle 477 fresh men went through the recruits' bombing course. And on December 26 and 27 the tests were carried out with the battalion bombers, for the purpose of granting the Bombers' Badge. These tests were now made much more difficult to pass, and only seven men passed the throwing and firing tests. After this period I never carried out any further instruction in the hand-grenade. The drafts later on came out more fully trained and the Battalion Bombing Officers carried on any further instruction that was required. During and in preparation for the operations on the Somme 16 officers and 2106 men went through the course; and at least 5000 live grenades were thrown. I was lucky to have no accident with the Mills grenade, and no fatal ones even with the rifle-grenade.

General Ovens went on leave at Bresle, and Lieut.-Col. G. Scott Jackson, O.C. 7th N.F., came as Brigade Commander to our H.Q. We had him several times again in that capacity, and he was always a favourite in our mess. His fine record and services are well known; a D.S.O. and Bar, he probably commanded a fighting battalion as long as any officer in France. From the time when the battalion landed in France in April 1915 till he left the battalion for the R.A.M.C. at the latter end of 1917, he was only off duty for about three days, in a quiet part of the line. He always looked a picture of robust strength, never missed his cold bath even with the temperature near zero, and was one of the most optimistic men in the whole Brigade. He was a most pleasant kindly Brigade Commander, with the supreme virtue of leaving the specialists to do their work in their own way.

Before we left Bresle I got a Brigade Bombing Sergeant - Sergeant T. Matthewson of the 5th N.F., who had had long experience as Battalion Bombing Sergeant, and was a thoroughly trained and reliable man. I found him most useful in his new office and I am glad to know that he got safely through the war. Amongst other accomplishments he was a good wicket-keeper, as I found later on.

On Christmas Day I went to dinner with the 7th N.F. at their H.Q., and was very hospitably entertained. The Brigade moved from Bresle to a camp at Bécourt on November 28, and stayed there two days; and then took over from a Brigade of the 1st Division at Bazentin-le-Petit.

CHAPTER XIX

BUTTE OF WARLENCOURT - TRENCH WARFARE

ON DECEMBER 30, 1916, the Brigade was in the reserve area about Bazentin-le-Petit, and ready to take over the line of trenches running eastwards from a point south of the Butte of Warlencourt. No material change had taken place on this part of the front since the fruitless attack of November 11. The 1st Division, however, had done a good deal of work in the back areas, and had laid duck-board tracks from High Wood to the front line, and increased the number of light railways. B.H.Q. were at some dugouts at the 'Cough Drop,' a place about a mile north of High Wood. The 149th Infantry Brigade had now decided to make use of a party of 'Observers,' and Major Anderson asked me to take charge of them. I was a little diffident about this as I had never had any experience as a Battalion Intelligence Officer and really knew nothing at all about observation. But I was glad to take on the job, and I soon got to like it. On December 30, therefore, two trained observers from each of the four battalions of the Brigade reported to me. And I had two N.C.Os. with this party - a corporal of the 4th N.F., who soon left to take a commission, and L.-C. Amos of the 7th N.F., who afterwards became N.C.O. in charge. On the same day I met the Intelligence Officer of the 1st Brigade who took me over the line and showed me the two O.P.s. I was lucky to meet at the start an officer who understood the business so well. He gave me many useful hints, and handed over an excellent panoramic sketch map of the view from one O.P., as well as the Log Book. The latter was a notebook containing reports of every movement of the enemy seen from the O.P.s. On December 31 I took the party of observers up to the Cough Drop where they had a shelter near B.H.Q. I had also supervision of the two Brigade dumps, one at Hexham Road and the other at the Flers Line about half a mile north of B.H.Q. Both places came in for heavy shelling at intervals all day and night, for both were situated about the end of a trench tramway, an obvious place for dumping stores. However I had the latter dump moved to a better place, some distance from the tramway, where there was less scrap iron lying about. During this tour in the line which lasted eight days, I was employed in looking after the observers and the two Brigade bomb stores. Towards the close of our stay I started to make a new bomb store in Hexham Road. Capt. H. Liddell gave me the general design of it and told me what materials I should require. But I had no more time than to get the emplacement dug out and the wooden framework erected.[13] I remember that we struck two buried Germans in excavating the emplacement and had to treat them with some very powerful corrosive before the work could be continued.

Also it was rather a warm corner in Hexham Road, and I caught a shell splinter on the leg; this, however, struck the steel buckle on my trench boot and only raised a bruise. The weather became very cold towards the end of our stay, with snow and frost. The Germans opposite our trenches were not disposed to be unfriendly about the New Year. On the left near the Butte they signalled to our men in the trenches before a trench-mortar bombardment started, as if to warn them to take cover. On the right they were still more inclined to fraternise. Here both sides were holding trenches that would have become impossible if any sniping had been done. So both our men and the Germans worked away at deepening their own trenches without molesting their opponents; although sometimes a crowd of men were exposed from the waist upwards at a range of about 200 yards.

It was one of those curious understandings which arise when no violent operations are in progress. However, on New Year's Day it went

13. Pte. Slack (7th N.F.), a Brigade pioneer, helped me greatly with the carpenter's work.

even further. A soldier of the 5th N.F., after signals from the Germans, went out into No Man's Land and had a drink with a party of them. After this a small party of the enemy approached our trenches without arms and with evidently friendly intentions. But they were warned off and not allowed to enter our trenches. This little affair, I believe, led to the soldier being court-martialled for holding intercourse with the enemy. After eight days in the line the Brigade returned to a camp at the north end of Mametz Wood. B.H.Q. were close to a battery of 9-inch howitzers, and when these heavy guns fired a salvo, which they did occasionally both day and night, it fairly lifted the things off the table. We got shelled here one night, but beyond getting a shower or two of splinters and stones on to the huts no damage was done. I had now time to ramble round, and examine various things of interest. I found a regular dump of German bombs at Bazentin-le-Grand, and some of these were collected for training purposes.

There were some Divisional baths at Bazentin-le-Petit, and I remember having a most cold and miserable bath there one night; but it was better than none at all. It was surprising how quickly the heavy railway had been brought along. It now reached High Wood, but of course did not cross the ridge, which would have been in view of the enemy. About January 15 we went back to the line in very cold weather, and B.H.Q. stayed at the Cough Drop again for eight days. During this time I set to work completing the bomb store at Hexham Road, and filling it with grenades. Each morning I got a party of about sixteen men, and we collected a lot of filled sandbags to pack round the framework and shed which were soon finished. The Brigade observers held a post in the old Flers Line, from which good observation was obtained on the ground between Loupart Wood and Grevillers. It was not difficult to get the heavy gunners to fire on German working-parties that were spotted by the observers; and several parties were duly dispersed by our shells. Before we left the line this time, the Brigade bomb store at Hexham Road was completed and filled. And when I visited the district again in June 1917 it was still standing. I also began now to write out the Brigade Intelligence Reports which were sent in each day, and contained a summary of the events that had happened or had been observed on our front. On January 23 we went back to the camp north of Mametz Wood.

After a few days we moved off to Albert, and stayed two or three days in a house near the railway line. The town got both bombed and shelled at times, though not very severely. After this we moved off to the village of Dernancourt for a short rest.

Major C.G. Johnson, M.C., who was adjutant of the 7th N.F. when I joined the battalion, was now attached to B.H.Q. as Assistant-Staff-Captain. He was an exceedingly able man, and had a good knowledge of military law. We all liked him well as adjutant of the battalion, and our relations at B.H.Q. were always friendly. He left us eventually to become D.A.Q.M.G. in a higher Staff formation.

CHAPTER XX

FRANCE AND THE FRENCH

THE WAR HAS done at least one thing for me. It has opened my eyes and changed my views with regard to the French. I confess that once I had no liking for them and a certain measure of contempt. I suppose the average Englishman has started with views like these. There has been bad blood between the two races, and that at no very distant date. Indeed the Alliance or Entente started much like a marriage of convenience. The two partners were joined in interest together against a common foe and a common danger.

Personally, I do not think there was much love lost between the two nations for some time after the war started. The bond of mutual admiration and respect, and I hope of affection, was forged in the Battle of the Somme and in the heroic defence of Verdun. This bond has been strengthened since on many a stricken field. The clouds of mutual mistrust and jealousy have been largely dispelled. We have learnt much about the French since the early days of the war, and they much about us; otherwise it would have been impossible for a French General to be in supreme command of the campaign.

I have often come in contact with the French civilian in town and country, but only rarely with French troops. Also I have come to know and like a series of French interpreters attached to battalions or brigade. The deeds of the French Army speak for themselves, and their Staff work has been often beyond praise. When we remember the cruel fate that befell the north-eastern corner of France and its unhappy citizens, we may sympathise with the fury of the French nation against their old oppressors. No one living in England can realise the hideous wounds inflicted on this fair country-side. It may explain to some extent at least the heroic resistance of the French for over four years - a resistance that could scarcely have been predicted before the war.

In considering our relations with the French at different times, it is well to have a deep sympathy for the cruel wrongs she has suffered. Thus they must have regarded with very mixed feelings their harbours, railways, and towns being taken over by an alien though friendly people.

All things considered the Frenchman may well have said at the first, 'These English, they are everywhere!' At least, this I noticed when I arrived in Le Havre in January 1916, there was no enthusiasm for us there. There was no rudeness, it is true, but the atmosphere of the place was rather chilly and aloof. The country folk about Meteren seemed pleased to see us; I think they had got used to the ways of the British soldier and found him not such a bad fellow after all. It was pleasant to see the country folks round here after our stay in Flanders, comely and straight, members of a thoroughbred race. The contrast was rather forcible perhaps.

The Brigade Interpreter in 1916, Monsieur Bunge, a native of Le Havre, was a pleasant, lively sort of person, always ready for a joke and an admirer of the British. With him I got on very well; and I learnt one or two things of the French from him. One of them was how sensitive they are in small matters of conversation. If in your heavy English way you did not respond at once with animation to his remarks, M. Bunge thought he had offended you.

They are a very sensitive race, especially in matters of courtesy. The colder manner and bearing of the British must have been a sore trial to them till they got to understand them - especially if they were laying themselves out to be friendly. It is worth while to let yourself go a bit in the matter of speech and bearing when talking to them. And, above all things, if you want to please them, try to talk to them in French, however badly, for they all take it as a great compliment. Another thing I discovered was the unwillingness of the French officers to take the initiative in saluting; yet they would never fail to return such a courtesy. Perhaps their earlier experiences in this little matter had been discouraging. It is much the same with the poilus and farmer folk. If you wish them 'Bonjour' they would invariably respond and also salute.

Later on I had a day or two in Amiens which provided some impressions of the French soldiers. The officers there contrasted rather forcibly with our own, I remember. They were very smartly dressed in home-parade uniforms, wore their medals, and carried themselves with an admirable pride and spirit. Our officers, on the other hand, dressed in the homely khaki, often the worse for wear, had generally an air of war-weariness. No doubt most of our men had come almost straight from the battle-field and were enjoying only a few hours' relaxation in this fine city. Still it made one reflect that the French are indeed a nation of soldiers which we are not. We obviously have not the same pride in the paraphernalia of war, and that shows which way the wind blows. I also saw a number of poilus going on leave and returning to the line. They looked very quiet and patient, but without a great deal of enthusiasm showing on the surface. Later on I saw French soldiers on the march several times. They get over the ground very fast; but it is more go as you please with them than with us. I have often noticed how grave these poilus look, even after the war was over. Nothing of the reckless fun and explosive good humour of the British soldier. If the latter is not having a rotten time he is wonderfully cheerful and often light-hearted.

I have also seen the French soldiers holding the line in a quiet part; and indeed we 'took over' from them there. They do not expose themselves nearly so much as we do near the trenches. Everything seemed to be done with scientific method and every one seemed to know exactly what to do on all occasions. They hold their front line thinly, trusting in case of accidents to recover it by a counter-attack. And if the French are not fighting a battle they generally keep their front as quiet as they can. This of course is all very different from our own system. If we had a quiet part of the line, it was generally because we had silenced the enemy's guns and trench-mortars by fighting.

I had one great chance of studying the French officer at home in these trenches. Shortly before taking over the French Regimental Commander in the line asked our Brigadier, Brigade-Major, and 'one other officer' to visit the trenches, but to be sure and call in at Regimental H.Q. before proceeding up the line. This was really an invitation of goodwill and ceremony rather than an invitation to examine the line. But as this was not quite understood at the time I was included in the party as Brigade Bombing Officer, rather than the Staff-Captain or Machine-Gun Officer, either of whom should have gone in my place. So on a terribly cold day at the end of January 1917 we set off, and after a long ride from Dernancourt to Fontaine-les-Cappy in a motor-car, we arrived near Regimental H.Q. and proceeded there on foot. The Brigadier was a fair French linguist, I had about two words of French, and the Brigade-Major had none. So it was just as well that the junior État-Major happened to be a fluent English speaker. Indeed, he had spent a good time in Newcastle and knew not only England but the north. We were welcomed by the French Brigadier with every mark of courtesy and goodwill. It is the custom for a French officer to salute his superior and then to shake hands with him. The salute is given even if you do not happen to be wearing a cap.

These worthy and hospitable warriors were in charge of a regiment (or as we should say a brigade) from the south of France about Bordeaux. I believe they had won for themselves a good reputation as fighting men. They knew, however, as well how to take care of themselves; and I fancy they had a first-class chef amongst their servants. It was a great affair, that meal, which had been prepared to do us honour, especially considering that it was served actually in the trenches. Quite a number of dishes succeeded one another, and were washed down with some excellent red wine. These were followed by several sweets and a glass of sweet champagne - the latter to drink to our good luck in the new trenches - glasses were solemnly clinked at this stage of the proceedings; afterwards cognac, coffee and cigars. The French officers expressed considerable interest in the Territorial 'T.'s' on my tunic, asking what they stood for. The French 'Territorial' is of course a different type to ours, being in the nature of the last reserve, elderly men not used as 'storm' or 'shock' troops. The meal passed pleasantly indeed; and at the end, a photograph must be taken as a souvenir of the meeting, and that was duly done in the winter sunlight outside. The French soldiers use small cameras in the trenches, a privilege denied to us. I have never before or since been in such elaborate trenches as these that we took over from the French. Vast communication trenches, six to ten feet deep, ran back for miles behind the front line. The same with the forward area, the number of deep trenches was simply extraordinary. Their idea may have been to make so many trenches that the enemy would not know which to shell. Unfortunately the trenches were not revetted, and when the frost broke we came to think less of them and travelled as much as possible across the open. The inside of the trenches was very clean - not a tin or a scrap of paper to be seen. The refuse was all dumped just over the parapet or in the shell-holes outside. The French are accustomed to an easy system of sanitation. During the day few French soldiers are seen outside their dugouts, except parties cleaning the trenches. In the front line only a few sentries were kept on duty, and they were relieved every two hours. The French speak with great confidence of their field artillery, the terrible 75's. A battery of these guns handled by French gunners can fire almost like a machine-gun, and the noise is deafening.

As a nation the French have their faults. They are exceedingly proud and quick to take offence, they are not very stable or constant (obstinate shall we say?), and they are about the hardest bargainers in the world.

Thrift and making use of the shining hour have been driven to their last conclusions. The British soldiers have been made to pay very sweetly for their visit to France. I do not think the French ever gave the British such a warm welcome as the Belgians did.

But when all is said and done we all have our own faults, and the Frenchman's most shining virtue is patriotism.

CHAPTER XXI

SOUTH OF THE SOMME

AFTER STAYING FOR about a week or more at Dernancourt, the Brigade received orders to go south of the Somme, and to take over part of the line won by the French this side of Peronne. We marched, therefore, through Bray and stayed two nights at Mericourt and two at Fontaine-les-Cappy. At the latter place I was surprised to find some graves of British soldiers who had fallen there in the earlier part of the war. Also I had one exciting experience at Fontaine-les-Cappy. There was a large grenade dump near our camp, and, just as I was passing it, an explosion took place. A party of men had been detonating grenades, and two or three grenades had gone off in the box, killing two of the party and hurling the grenades in a shower all round the place. One fell close, and I was lucky not to be riddled by it. For the safety-pin was blown out and the lever of the grenade held down by a piece of wood from the side of the box, which was jammed by the explosion into the shoulder of the grenade. I spent a little time picking up such grenades as I could find, and two or three of them were in a dangerous condition.

When we got into the line near Belloy I lived for a time at advanced B.H.Q. called 'P.C. Hedevaux' ('Post Commandant' *Hedevaux*). The dugouts were deep and proof against ordinary shells. The General, Brigade-Major, and Staff-Captain resided farther back at 'P.C. Buelow.' I was shown over the trenches by the *officier bombardier* (Bombing Officer) of a French unit. And I found it fairly easy to talk to him without the aid of an interpreter. I told him two English expressions which seemed to please him greatly. One was 'dugout,' the other 'dump'; the equivalent for the latter in French being 'Depôt de Munitions.'

I made an entirely new Brigade bomb store in these trenches, using the little shelters in a line of disused trenches. After a week in the trenches the frost broke, and the trenches which had been hard and dry now became nothing but muddy drains. To wade along them even in daylight and in gum boots involved the greatest physical exertion. One unfortunate man stuck in the mud, and before they got him out he was pulled out of his boots and breeches and had his coat torn off his back. Finally he was sent to the dressing-station with only his shirt on. We stayed about sixteen days in the line, and during the last five or six days I retired to P.C. Buelow to assist in the Intelligence Work.

This part of the line was quiet and our stay uneventful; but two things of interest might be noted. The Brigade observers reported that the Germans were employing French prisoners on the roads about a mile behind their front line, a cowardly and disgraceful proceeding. The Germans were seen working hard on their dugouts behind the line - this was of course a 'blind' for our benefit, for the German retreat started the day after the 50th Division was relieved.

After our sixteen days in the line B.H.Q. moved back to Foucaucourt and remained there till about March 7. Then the 50th Division finally left the Somme front and moved back for a rest. B.H.Q. went to Warfusée and we had good billets there.

Brigadier-General Ovens, C.M.G., left us at Foucaucourt and Lieut.-Col. B.D. Gibson, D.S.O., of the 4th N.F., commanded the Brigade for a few days, being succeeded as Brigade Commander by Lieut.-Col. G. Scott Jackson, D.S.O., of the 7th N.F.

Two very startling things were done at this time. All the men of the Brigade were told that they were about to be trained for open warfare, and they would not have to go into the trenches again. They were to be used as part of a Corps de Chasse during the next offensive. This was not borne out by events, but it throws some light on the expectations of the British Staff. It was also decided at this juncture to change the organisation of the British Infantry Company. Each company was in future to consist of four sections - one riflemen pure and simple, another Lewis gunners, another bombers, and the fourth rifle-bombers.

It was perhaps an unfortunate time to spring this change on the B.E.F., just on the eve of a new offensive. The idea appears to have been sound enough, but the attempt to rush it through in three weeks' time was hardly likely to have good results. To convert a rifleman into a rifle-bomber in a week's training was of course out of the question. Hitherto only the most expert and steadiest bombers had been employed on rifle-grenade work. But now the ordinary infantry were expected to become rifle-bombers, although their knowledge of bombs was of the most elementary description. Two problems therefore faced those responsible for the training and equipment of the rifle-bombers. First how to get them even partially trained in the time, and second to invent some apparatus for carrying the rifle-grenades. At first it was only possible to train the N.C.O.s in charge of the rifle-bombing sections - leaving them to instruct their sections as well as they could.

It is hard to realise the complete inadequacy of this arrangement, without knowing something of the rifle-grenade, and without knowing the extraordinary difficulty of training a man to become an instructor of others. However that was the best that could be made of the new orders at the moment. And so it fell to me to take a class for a week of N.C.O'.s drawn from the four battalions. I had not only to teach them to fire the rifle-grenade themselves, of which they knew nothing, but to teach them to hand their knowledge on to others.

The training went on from March 12 to 17, and thirty-four section leaders attended the course. About 1150 rounds were fired. I did not attempt any live firing - in fact, I have never thought it serves any useful purpose to fire live rifle-grenades in practice.

It is of course much more dangerous than throwing a live hand-grenade, and one accident in practice is enough to discourage all the recruits who see it from firing live rifle-grenades in actual warfare. On the other hand, even where the rifle-grenades are only used as dummies, the waste of valuable ammunition is simply appalling. A Hales rifle-grenade used to cost 25s. and it came down to 15s. a little later, but once fired as a dummy it was not much use to fire again. Dummies could have been made for about 1s. at the most, but of course no one in England thought about a trifle like that; and so the colossal waste went on all the time I had the training in hand. I did what I could by straightening the rods to use the grenades again, but I could not save much in this way. Thousands of pounds in rifle-grenades must have been used where thousands of shillings should have been spent.

At Warfusée Brigadier-General H.C. Rees, D.S.O., came to take over command of the Brigade. He had seen very heavy fighting in the early part of the war, and had since commanded two Brigades before he came to the 149th Infantry Brigade. He was liked and respected by every one in the Brigade. Very tall and well built, and a soldier who gave you the greatest confidence in his ability and leadership, the Brigade owed much to him, especially at a time when the trench fighting was giving way (as it seemed) to open warfare. He was a first-class rifle-shot himself, and never ceased to impress the necessity of developing this weapon to the utmost. For the hand-grenade he had the greatest contempt, which he was rather fond of expressing. Fortunately for me, bombing work was giving way to Intelligence, although for some time to come I had to train the men in rifle grenades and to look after the Brigade ammunition stores.

After finishing the rifle-grenade work I acted as Assistant-Staff-Captain for about a week. It was chiefly office work as far as I was concerned, the returns being very voluminous. Work as I could there seemed to be no getting to the end of these returns till 9 or 10 o'clock at night. There were also one or two minor court-martial cases, in which my legal training proved some assistance. On March 27 I got my third leave granted, for ten days. It was perhaps rather quick after my last leave, but the fact of my being ill on that occasion was taken into consideration. This time I went to Amiens by motor-lorry and thence to Boulogne, reaching Manchester on the same day that I sailed from France.

On April 6 I left Folkestone and got to Boulogne about 4 o'clock. Here no one could say where the 56th Division was, and I was directed to leave by a midnight train and to report to the R.T.O. at Abbéville. I got there about 2 A.M. and was told to go back to Étaples by an 8 o'clock train that morning. I managed to get a few hours' sleep and breakfast at the Officers Club at Abbéville, and reached Étaples about midday on April 7. On April 9 I was told to proceed to St. Pol and get further directions there. I arrived there in time for lunch, and then reached Frévent by another train. Here I was told to go by the light railway towards Wanquetin and to make inquiries for the 50th Division on the way. At Frévent I saw a lot of slightly wounded soldiers coming back from Arras; they had been over the top that morning on the first day of the great battle which had just started. Just before reaching Avesnes-le-Compte I spotted some Divisional transport on the roads, and, on making inquiries at Avesnes, I learnt that the 149th Infantry Brigade were quartered at Manin about two miles away. So I left the train and reached our H.Q. just in time for dinner.

The 50th Division had marched from Warfusée, and were now proceeding towards Arras to take part in the battle which had started on April 9.

CHAPTER XXII

THE BATTLE OF ARRAS

THE BATTLE OF Arras started with a great success. The Vimy Ridge was recaptured and the vast fortress between Telegraph Hill and Neuville Vitasse, including a substantial part of the famous Hindenburg Line, fell in one day. The high ground at Monchy-le-Preux was soon stormed and secured. But after this progress became very slow, nothing seemed to come of these great tactical successes. The fighting, instead of developing into open warfare as we had expected, became again very similar in character to the great trench to trench battles on the Somme.

The French waited a week before starting their offensive in Champagne, and when it did start it failed completely. The weather broke down on April 10, as it generally did in 1917 whenever the British commenced offensive operations. It became very cold and it rained or snowed almost incessantly for over a week. It is hard for one who saw only a small sector of this great battle to understand what prevented us from taking greater advantage of our great initial success, which certainly surprised and disorganised the enemy. But it was not merely the weather which broke down at a critical moment. There were other causes at work to delay and impede success. I strongly suspect that the British infantry units were still suffering from their tremendous exertions in 1916; and they certainly had not the confident assurance of victory which inspired the terrible sacrifices on the Somme. Hitherto our artillery had never been so strong nor had the mechanical aids to victory been so numerous or so varied. Gas-projectors and oil-drums were first used in this battle, new aeroplanes were first launched out in public; the British held the mastery of the air, and the Germans had not yet devised any effective remedy for the British tanks. But the British troops were not the troops of the Somme. The old type of volunteer had largely disappeared, and the same resolution and confidence were not displayed by some of the British divisions. The very strength of our artillery was sapping the old reliance on the rifle, and when the barrage stopped the infantry often seemed to be powerless to defend the captured positions.

On the other hand the superior and more lengthy training of the German reserves now began to tell. Personally, I never admired the German as a fighting man until he was now for the first time driven out of his vast defences. On the Somme the Germans had artillery support nearly equal to our own, and they were defending superb trenches with unbroken roads and country behind them. Now, when they were thrust out of their famous stronghold and plastered with every sort of projectile, they held up repeated attacks, backed by enormous artillery preparation and support, held them up by sheer dogged fighting and superior knowledge of war. Their Staff work must have been good, and the training and morale of the troops equally good to have done it. After the first great success, we gained only small local successes, costing thousands of casualties and vast expenditure of ammunition. Eventually, after about five weeks of fierce thrusts, the Battle of Arras came to an end, giving us, it is true, a much improved position in front of Arras, but leaving the main object of the attack unaccomplished. The further offensives of 1917 were carried on more to the north and south, and the Arras area saw no more big fighting till the beginning of 1918.

The 50th Division came into action on April 11, and worked alternately with the 14th Division. The enemy were pushed across the Cojeul Valley and into the outskirts of Vis-en-Artois and Cherisy. The advance of these two Divisions would have been undoubtedly greater, but Guemappe on the left and the uncaptured part of the Hindenburg Line on the right for a time held up the divisions attacking on either flank. Thus both the 50th Division and the 14th Division captured Cherisy in turn, but had to abandon the place through having their flanks exposed. By their operations in this area both Divisions maintained their already worthy reputation.

CHAPTER XXIII

WANCOURT TOWER - CROISILLES

THE 149TH INFANTRY Brigade left Manin on the morning of April 10, and marched to Wanquetin, where the troops were billeted in houses. On the following day it began to snow heavily about midday and this continued far into the night. The Brigade were intended to attack on April 12, but, owing to the exhaustion and exposure of the troops, the 151st Brigade were substituted when the attack recommenced on April 13. We started our march in the snow just as the light was beginning to fail, and trudged along through the muddy slush till we reached Arras. Here there was a delay of several hours before guides arrived to lead the various units to their stations. B.H.Q. marched through the town and eventually arrived at the ruined sugar factory at Faubourg Ronville, where there were deep dugouts below the ruins. We could not see much of the city but it appeared to be badly knocked about by the enemy's shells. Not many houses, perhaps, had fallen to bits, but there was hardly a house that had not been hit. A great many small shells must have been fired into the town. The place of course was full of underground passages - though I never had the chance of entering them. When morning came I was able to take stock of my surroundings. The sugar factory was one of the last buildings at the S.E. end of the city, and a trench tramway led to what had once been the front line trenches about a quarter of a mile from these H.Q.

My job that morning was to hunt round for the dumps of grenades &c. which had been made by our predecessors before their advance. I remember finding two of these in fairly good condition in the neighbourhood of Telegraph Hill - only of course on the Arras side.

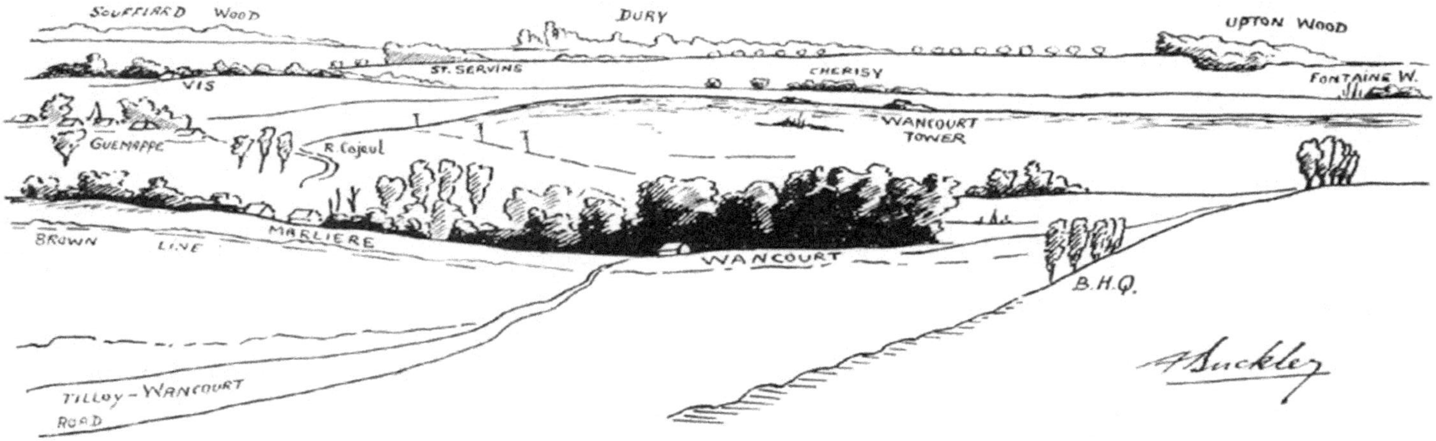

Scene of Attacks on Cherisy. April 1917.

The cold night on which we arrived had taken heavy toll of the cavalry horses, and many of these splendid animals could be seen scattered about on the ground, some already dead and others dying. They were too fine bred to stand that wintry night in an open bivouac. As far as I could make out our lighter siege guns had moved up towards the Telegraph Hill ridge and our field guns towards Neuville Vitasse; there were still howitzers of heavy calibre in the environs of the city itself. I believe the 151st Infantry Brigade attacked on April 13, and pushed across the Cojeul Valley north of Héninel, and dug in just west of the Wancourt Tower ridge. Wancourt was captured but not Guemappe, and Marlière was in our hands. On that day I was instructed to make a dump at Telegraph Hill, which I had no difficulty in doing as the place was quite quiet.

The next day this dump was removed to the region of the Elm Trees at Wancourt behind the 'Brown Line'; and the Brigade relieved the 151st Infantry Brigade. B.H.Q. were at the Elm Trees, and consisted of some fine deep dugouts, which the Germans had used as an ammunition store. The entrance to them was in a small sunken road. The ammunition was mostly stored in large wooden boxes, and we had to pull it out and get rid of it. This was done by emptying the boxes into the nearest shell-holes; so that the ground outside was littered with German ammunition. In one of these shell-holes, amongst a lot of rubbish of this kind, I found four old pewter dishes and two pewter spoons. They had been heaved out of the dugout along with the rest of its contents. One of the plates was dated 1733, and all were marked with the foreign maker's stamp. They afforded, when cleaned, a rather unusual decoration for the walls of the mess room. This little collection was disposed of 'under Divisional and Brigade arrangements,' but I managed to secure the spoons.

The position in front was now as follows. A battalion held the trenches across the Cojeul Valley, supported by three battalions in the Brown Line and in Wancourt itself. The enemy was in Guemappe and also in some trenches just over the ridge of Wancourt Tower Hill. It was the business of the Brigade to hold the trenches and to make such improvement in them as opportunity might offer. General Rees was not the man to let any such opportunity slip. Nothing happened during the first few days, beyond the usual heavy shelling of the roads and batteries and forward positions.

But a patrol of the 5th N.F. pushed out towards Guemappe, and carried out a useful daylight reconnaissance.

Also about April 16, 1917, Lieut.-Col. F. Robinson of the 6th N.F. discovered the enemy approaching the ruined buildings on the Wancourt Tower Hill, and promptly ordered a platoon to attack them. This plan succeeded admirably and the Tower and house were captured. The place was of vital importance to us as it commanded direct observation on all the roads leading to our part of the front. On April 17 the enemy shelled the Tower with 8-inch howitzers - generally a sign that he meant to attack sooner or later. The Tower contained a formidable concrete machine-gun emplacement, facing of course our way, but by General Rees' orders it was blown up by the Engineers. Sure enough the enemy attacked the Tower that night, and at an unfortunate time for us, for the 7th N.F. were in the process of relieving the 6th N.F. in the front line, and it was a vile night, with a blizzard of snow.

The German attack succeeded in driving our men out of the Tower and buildings, and though several bombing attacks were made that night to recover the position it could not be done. General Rees at once prepared to storm the position at the earliest opportunity next day, the 7th N.F. having completed the relief of the trenches during the night. It is difficult to describe the confidence which our General inspired at this critical time; he was rather graver and more thoughtful than usual, perhaps, but he treated the matter with great confidence and made every one feel that the misfortune could and would be retrieved at the first attempt. His plans were made in conjunction with Major Johnson of the 50th Divisional Artillery; and as a result it was arranged to attack across the open supported by a barrage from five brigades of field artillery. The hour was fixed for twelve noon (German time) just when the enemy is thinking about his dinner. Without any preliminary bombardment, the barrage opened out at the appointed hour, and fairly drove the enemy off the hill top. The 7th N.F. advanced in perfect order and with little opposition recaptured the Tower and the neighbouring trenches. Two or three prisoners were sent down, who had been unable to get away before the attackers reached them. It was a little attack, but carried out with admirable precision and practically without loss, and every credit must be given to General Rees for the way he handled the problem. As this operation was carried out in full view of all the surrounding country it attracted considerable attention, and congratulations soon poured in from all sides. I was kept indoors or rather underground a good deal during this stay in the line, as it was my business to record in a log-book every note or message that came in to the Brigade Office, either by day or night. I had the chance, too, of hearing the Divisional Intelligence Officer examining a few German prisoners who were captured on our front. He brought with him three large books containing no doubt the previous history of the German Brigades; and with the aid of these he was able to check the accuracy of the prisoners' statements.

One day I went with General Rees to Marlière, and we went some distance down Southern Avenue, which was then between the German outpost line and our own. Another day we went to some high ground N.W. of Wancourt for the purposes of observation. I remember that on this occasion we had to hurry as the Germans were shelling rather close, and General Rees got a splinter on the helmet. We were relieved by the 150th Infantry Brigade on April 21, and I rode back to Arras with Capt. Haggie. I was now billeted for two days in a house in Arras, where the Brigade Staff-Captain's office was located. The first night was quiet enough, but the following night was not so pleasant. For our heavy guns were now bombarding the German positions and their long-range guns threw a lot of shells in reply into various parts of the city. On April 23, St. George's Day, the British resumed the attack and the 150th Infantry Brigade attacked from the top of Wancourt Tower Hill. A good number of prisoners were made, but Guemappe still held out and the Germans launched a heavy counter-attack along this part of the front. In the morning I went forward to some dugouts east of Telegraph Hill where the General, Brigade-Major, and Signalling Officer were stationed for this battle. Our Brigade of course was in reserve, except the 4th N.F.

who were attached to the 151st Infantry Brigade. From this place near Telegraph Hill I got a good view of the battle around Guemappe. About midday Brigadier-General Cameron of the 151st Infantry Brigade took over command of the 50th Divisional front, and at once made preparations to renew the attack in the afternoon. I was sent over to the Elm Trees dugouts to find out exactly what he proposed to do with the 4th N.F., and he was then busily engaged with the Artillery officers arranging the barrages. Before the attack was resumed, Guemappe was heavily shelled by our siege guns, a wonderful sight. The whole place seemed to disappear in dense clouds of dust and smoke. It had been a ding-dong battle all day, attack and counter-attack, and at this point neither side had gained much advantage. The Germans had not only repelled the attack on our right, but had attempted to push through into Héninel, in the Cojeul Valley. Fortunately, however, the 149th M.-G. Company, commanded by Major Morris, stopped this movement by a well-directed fire to our right flank. When, however, the attack was renewed in the afternoon things went better for us. The Germans were pushed down the hill from Wancourt Tower and Guemappe was taken. The 4th N.F. did well, getting to a place called Buck Trench. And the Divisional front was advanced to a point not far from the outskirts of Cherisy. It was unfortunate that we had no fresh troops at this juncture to press home the attack. According to German statements, the German troops were practically broken up at the end of the day and they had at the moment no reserves available. Our small party remained at the H.Q. on Telegraph Hill till the morning of April 25, when we returned to the Ronville sugar factory, being relieved by a Brigade of the 14th Division.

On April 26 a large Corps dump about a quarter of a mile from the factory got on fire, and went on flaring and exploding all day. A good many pieces of shells and fragments from this dump came rattling against the walls of the sugar factory, making it no place to loiter about. I learnt that the 42nd F.A., to which my brother George was attached, was due to take over from our F.A. in Ronville; but I did not get in touch with him.

On April 26 B.H.Q. moved to a fine château at the west end of Arras, where we were much more comfortable than at the sugar factory. That night I went to a battalion dinner of the 7th N.F., and it was wonderful what a good dinner they managed to procure under the circumstances. The next day, April 27, we marched back to a rest area near Pommera, going along the Arras-Doullens road. B.H.Q. were billeted in a farm at the south end of the village. I shared a billet with Lieut. Odell and found the place very comfortable.

We were not left long here. A fresh attack was to be made, and the 50th Division was to be moved forward, to be ready to press home the attack if it succeeded. We left Pommera on May 1 and marched to Souastre, where B.H.Q. were billeted in a French château with a nice garden. Next day we marched forward again to a bare looking spot at Mereatel, where the accommodation was very limited. We managed to rig up a few wooden shelters and bivouacs amongst the ruins of the houses. This had been a nice village, but the Germans had blown down every house and cut down every tree before they left it. They had even destroyed the small fruit bushes in the gardens, an unnecessarily wanton act.

The big attack was arranged for May 3 and it was preceded by the usual heavy bombardment. But nothing came of it but heavy casualties, and it was decided to send the Division back to the rest area again. On the evening of May 3 I met a Colonel of the R.A.M.C., 14th Division, who told me that he had seen my brother George at Neuville Vitasse just two hours before, and that he was quite well. I got this information, just too late, as we were now under orders to move back to the rest area. And on May 4 I marched back with the B.H.Q. transport to Souastre, and on May 5 to Pommera.

For the next ten days the Brigade carried out various tactical exercises under the directions of General Rees. One day was given to field firing practice, on which occasion I acted as one of the 'casualty' officers - that is to say, I had to select various men during the sham attack and order them to drop out as casualties. Live ammunition was used in rifles and Lewis guns as well as live rifle-grenades; and I remember there were seven slight casualties from accidents with the rifle-grenades. These 'live' field days in France were not without their own little excitements, especially for those who had to keep up with the firing line.

After ten days the Brigade was detached from the 50th Division and attached to the 33rd Division, holding the line about Croisilles. The idea was to assist the 33rd Division by holding the line for them for three days, in the interval between two attacks. So on May 17 the Brigade moved from Pommera to Souastre, H.Q. being again at the French château. Here, through the good services of our French interpreter, we had for dinner a piece of the famous *sanglier* which lives in the woods at Pommera. One of these creatures had been shot, and the huntsmen presented a piece of it to B.H.Q. Mess. It tasted much like pork, with a more gamy flavour.

On May 18 we moved from Souastre to Boiry St. Martin, where B.H.Q. were in some wooden huts, amongst the ruins of the village. On May 19 I went over to Ayette, a neighbouring village, and spent the morning training men of the 7th N.F. in rifle-grenades. Next day I went with Capt. Haggie to inspect a Brigade ammunition dump at Croisilles, and on May 21 I went to a canvas camp at Hamlincourt and spent the night there. I did not get a good night as the enemy shelled the vicinity of the camp at intervals during the night. Next day I went forward to B.H.Q. which were in some shelters in a sunken road just west of Croisilles. We held the line till May 25 and nothing very startling happened. But two or three incidents occurred here which I remember with interest. The visit of three War Correspondents, including Messrs. Beach Thomas and Philip Gibbs. They spent about half an hour at our H.Q. and were put in my charge to see the sights. We did not go far from H.Q. as the high ground there afforded the best general view of the country round.

Both of the English War Correspondents interested me much. Beach Thomas, tall and dignified and grave; Philip Gibbs, short and bright and cheery: both very sympathetic to and appreciative of the Brigade. The other was a Dutch gentleman who told me with a flash of inspiration that I should not recollect his name.

Another striking personality appeared in the shape of the Brigade Commander of one of the Divisional Artillery Brigades. Col. Fitzgerald came to call on us to inquire whether the artillery arrangements were to our satisfaction and to know if he could do anything to help us. A tall man with glasses and a kindly, gentle face. One morning he brought in a great bunch of flowers for our mess room that he had gathered near Croisilles. The following story was brought to us by the Artillery Liaison Officer. Col. Fitzgerald went to the front line and out into the broken trenches in No Man's Land in order to inspect the registration of the field guns. Seeing a German sniper at work, he borrowed a rifle and commenced a duel with the Boche in which several shots were exchanged. Having killed his man he returned with great satisfaction, feeling the day had been well spent. This occurred near the 'Hump' whilst we were holding these trenches. He told us that his guns had had a wonderful target on the Somme in July 1916. They were somewhere on the high ground south of Bazentin-le-Grand when the German Guard had massed for an attack on Contalmaison. These guns had the extraordinary chance of firing with open sights on the dense German masses behind Bazentin-le-Petit and they had inflicted terrible losses on the Brandenburghers.

It was from our O.P. near B.H.Q. that I first tried to make a panoramic sketch of the country in front. It was a crude attempt, no doubt, but General Rees was kind enough to speak encouragingly of it, and to tell me to try and develop this side of Intelligence.

That advice bore fruit, for in 1918 my observers were trained to sketch, and their sketches did more damage to the enemy than any reports that were sent in. For the heavy artillery got interested in them and fired on the targets with great effect.

About May 25 we came out of the line and stayed one night at Moyenneville, returning next day to our Divisional rest area at Monchy-au-Bois.

CHAPTER XXIV
MONCHY-AU-BOIS

WE WERE NOW able to settle down to training and manoeuvres. The country round Monchy was well suited for this, for there were many old German trenches about, and the villages were all smashed to bits, giving a realistic touch to field training. B.H.Q. were under canvas, but I selected an old German dugout which I thought would be drier when the rains set in. It was also cooler in the hot weather, and its only drawback was rats. I kept them in check, however, with a small trap that the Germans left behind; they were always good at inventing killing machines. My own job was now to train as many infantry men as possible in the use of the rifle-grenade. And between May 29 and June 16, 190 men went through the course. Also Lieut. Odell brought his signal company of twenty-nine men one evening to be shown the working of the rifle-grenade, as it was thought that the rifle-grenade (empty) might be used as a message carrier.

The course of instruction was somewhat as follows. In the first place I gave a short lecture on the mechanism of the grenade and methods of firing it. Then the party of ten was split into two squads and firing practice took place. The men were trained to fire kneeling and lying, behind cover and without, and also out of a deep fire-trench. I was greatly assisted by Sergt. T. Matthewson, who was a really expert bomber, and by my orderly - L.-C. Fairclough. This training took all morning, and as far as I could judge the men were interested in the course and did their best to learn the intricacies of this new weapon. In the afternoon I was free to wander round and examine the surrounding country. It was of considerable interest, for it was part of the ground evacuated by the enemy when he retreated to the Hindenburg Line. The trenches were magnificently built, and revetted with wood or wattle-work, and provided with deep dugouts and concrete machine-gun emplacements. The latter were not only wonderfully strong, the forerunners of the German 'pill-box' - but sometimes wonderfully decorated with coats of arms and mottoes.

Very little equipment was left behind, and many of the dugouts were blown in before leaving. Some of the gun emplacements, too, were very cleverly concealed. The guns were kept in shelters in a line of reserve trenches and a set of dummy emplacements was dug out a little distance away for the benefit of our aeroplane observers.

It was an education in military engineering and fortification to walk round these wonderful defences. The wiring too was most ingenious and often carefully concealed in the hedges or ditches. Inside the gun shelters, you found that the gun was fixed on a central pivot and worked round a wooden platform with every degree carefully marked. Whilst on the walls stood a painted board with every barrage line and target carefully worked out, and the range and code call set out as well. The O.P. was sometimes in a high tree, with the ladders to get up and the telephone wires still remaining. It had been a quiet part of the line, and consequently the patient industry of the German had had full scope.

The 50th Division began to take over the line west of Cherisy and Vis about the middle of June; but only two brigades were in the front trenches together, and it was our turn to remain behind. On June 18 the Brigade moved from Monchy-au-Bois to Boisleux-au-Mont, where B.H.Q. were in a canvas camp. From June 20 to 23 I continued the rifle-grenade training. The recruit training was now practically over and these days were given to showing the handling of a rifle-grenade section in open warfare. Forty-one officers, nine N.C.O.'s and sixty-two men took part in these schemes. I had also two or three rather important court-martial cases to attend to during the evenings.

Before going back into the line I was given nine men to act as Brigade observers; the 6th N.F. sent L.-C. Chappell and Ptes. Wright and Hume; the 7th N.F. Ptes. Fail and Ewart; the 4th N.F. Pte. Brook and another; the 5th N.F. L.-C. Roxburgh, who had once been in the 7th N.F. and Pte. Garnett. Pte. Brook I found came from Meltham, only seven or eight miles from my own home. He was a typical lad from these parts, with the bright red face and the speech that I knew so well. Naturally I took an interest in him and I was sorry when he left us about the end of November 1917. He has come through the war safely, I am glad to say. Ptes. Fail and Ewart were destined to act as my observers both with this brigade and in the 42nd Division in 1918. And I cannot speak too highly of the excellent work done by Pte. Fail. Owing to exceptional eyesight he was a first-class counter-battery observer, and later on his skill with the pencil did the Germans a lot of damage. On this front he spotted the flash of a 4-inch gun battery that used to shell B.H.Q., with the result that the heavy gunners fired on this battery and silenced it completely.

I had also the services of L.-C. J. Cowen and Pte. J. King (both 7th N.F.) when the 50th Divisional observers were disbanded. Pte. King went shortly afterwards back to the battalion. But both these men did magnificent service in collecting intelligence during the remainder of the war.

CHAPTER XXV

TRENCH WARFARE - VIS-CHERISY FRONT

FROM JUNE TILL October 1917 the 50th Division held the line of trenches running from the Hindenburg Line west of Fontaine-lez-Croisilles to Cavalry Farm on the Arras-Cambrai Road. With heavy fighting going on in Flanders this was a comparatively quiet part of the front. Our trenches were good and got better every week, and the high ground about Wancourt Tower Hill gave us excellent observation on the enemy's country, especially towards the left. This part of the front was divided into two sectors, and they were held by two out of the three brigades. So that each brigade spent sixteen days in the line, and then eight days in the rest area about Neuville Vitasse. Also each brigade held in turn the trenches on the right, known as the Cherisy sector, and then the trenches on the left, known as the Vis sector.

My time was given to Intelligence in the line and to Salvage when out of the line.

Intelligence work included, selecting a convenient O.P. for the Brigade observers and arranging and supervising the method of holding it; making panoramic sketches for the observers; writing out the Brigade Intelligence Report between 10 A.M. and noon every day; supervising the work of the Battalion Intelligence Officers[14]; marking the Brigade Intelligence maps with all features of interest; studying and cataloguing the aeroplane photographs which came in large numbers every few days; destroying obsolete and useless documents (not a small part of my job either!); and sending to the Machine-Gun Officer,

14. Lieuts. O. Young (5th N.F.), Jessop (6th N.F.), and Richardson (7th N.F.).

Major Morris, every week the targets for indirect machine-gun fire at nights. Field work, i.e. actual observation and sketching, formed really a comparatively small part of my duties, though I tried to get up to the observation post once every day. The most important part was office work - and I had a fair-sized shelter at each Head-quarters, the walls covered with maps and the table loaded with aeroplane photographs and reports of all kinds.

Besides the Corps and Divisional Intelligence Reports which came in daily, there were Daily Reports from the two adjoining brigades, and generally a goodly sheaf of miscellaneous papers from the Army Intelligence Department. In this way a great deal of interesting information came into my hands, as to how things were going on; and I have never before or since been so well supplied with information as to what was going on and what was intended to take place. When out of the line, in a camp near Neuville Vitasse, I had to give the observers a certain amount of practical training in the use of the compass and protractor, and map reading. But after that I was free to do what I liked within reason, and I generally devoted my spare time to salvage. The observers often turned out to assist me in this, and Lieut. Odell on several occasions gave me most valuable assistance with his signallers and orderlies.

Salvage was left very much at this time to the discretion of the commanders of infantry units. Naturally when the soldier man got out of the line, he was not much inclined to do much salvaging on Army Account. Some of the transport officers made a specialty of it, and Capt. B. Neville of the 7th N.F., the prince of quartermasters, rescued tons of salvage of all kinds. I dare say, however, a good many things found their way into his own stores as well, for I never knew a quartermaster so well supplied as he. There were certain small parties of men employed at Divisional and Corps Salvage dumps, but they never seemed to me to take the job very seriously. Perhaps the officers in charge were not exactly the sort of men to hustle, or to see that their men got busy. Every one knows that there was a vast amount of waste, and that the Germans had this matter much better organised than we.

The Germans were particularly active against our field artillery on this front. Although we had the advantage of ground for most purposes, and could carry out infantry reliefs in daylight, there were few places satisfactory for concealing our field guns. They were mostly concentrated about Wancourt and Héninel, and these two places consequently received frequent and heavy punishment from the German heavies. It was well to keep your eyes and ears open when passing through these villages and not to linger there unnecessarily. The pieces from the German 8-inch shell carried a long way, and I had L.-C. Chappell wounded through the hand and sent down to hospital through a splinter that carried over a quarter of a mile. We saw a lot of the 50th Divisional R.F.A. about this time and a fine lot of fellows they were. On the left our H.Q. were next door to the B.H.Q. of the 251st Artillery Brigade, commanded by Lieut.-Col. Moss Blundell. I got to know and like him well, and he did everything he could to assist our brigade, and especially in matters of intelligence. Any news that he got he sent on to us at once and vice versa. I have never known the liaison between Field Artillery and Infantry more close or more effective than at this time.

One of the most important operations carried out by the 50th Division was a double raid and gas projection on September 15, 1917, and the following night. It was carried out by the 151st Infantry Brigade in the right sector, and at the time the 140th Infantry Brigade was holding the trenches on the left. I believe the 9th D.L.I, supplied the raiding parties. It was such a novel and effective raid that some account ought to be given of it. The scheme was to deceive the enemy as to the exact extent and nature of the attack. For this purpose a great many smoke-shells were fired to screen the operations from the enemy's observation. Also along the flanks of the actual raid a number of dummy figures were arranged to represent an attacking force and so to draw the enemy's fire away from the actual raiding parties. The dummies were put out in No Man's Land the night before, face downwards, and at the right moment they could be raised or lowered by means of ropes worked by the men in the trenches. Also a dummy tank was prepared and hauled forward 200 yards by means of ropes. The combination of smoke-shells and dummies was wonderfully effective, and the enemy reported that he had been attacked in great force and with tanks along a large part of this front.

What really happened was this. After a preliminary bombardment of great intensity by our guns and trench-mortars (including many thermite or flame-shells), about 2 P.M. three companies of the 9th D.L.I, dashed across and captured the German front and support lines covering Cherisy. They killed and captured a number of Germans without suffering many casualties themselves, and then returned at once to our own trenches. At the same time the dummies in No Man's Land were lowered again. After waiting five or six hours, another short bombardment started, the dummies were again raised and one company of the 9th D.L.I, dashed across into the same trenches and killed or captured more Germans. They then returned to our trenches and the dummies were again lowered. After dark our men went out and removed the dummies, so that the Germans never had a chance of discovering the ruse. The same night at 3 A.M. fifty cylinders of gas were projected over the German lines. This gas attack cost the Germans dear, probably more than the two raids, for the next day they were seen burying or removing large numbers of the men caught in the gas cloud. My own observers reported 200 gas casualties and the total number reported reached a figure between 300 and 400. Gas casualties were easily distinguished, as the Germans removed them in blankets slung between two men on a pole. Besides, as it happened, the gas cloud drifted north and caught the Germans during a relief nearly half a mile away from the scene of the two raids. For example, the Germans were burying dead all day in the neighbourhood of St. Roharts Factory, which is some distance from Cherisy. The German report of this operation showed that they had failed entirely to realise the nature of the attack. And a similar raid was repeated shortly afterwards near Monchy-le-Preux with great success. Our aeroplanes swooped down to 300 feet and took photographs of the first raid from that height. And I was lucky enough to secure some very interesting copies of these photographs, which showed our men crossing No Man's Land and entering the German trenches.

I got my fourth leave, ten days, about August 30 and travelled home via Boulogne and Folkestone. It was the first leave that took me out of the line, which it did for about four days. All the previous leaves had occurred during Divisional rests.

We were relieved in these trenches by the 51st Division about the beginning of October, and the 50th Division moved out of the line to the neighbourhood of Courcelles-le-Compte for a short rest.

Before the relief took place Brigadier-General Rees had to leave us much to every one's regret. He was taken ill with a distressing internal complaint, which necessitated his return for a while to England. He was succeeded by Brigadier-General E.P.A. Riddell, C.M.G., D.S.O.

General Riddell had at one time been Adjutant of the 7th N.F., that is to say, long before the war; and he knew all about Alnwick and the people there. During the war he had been instructing officers at Sandhurst for a time, and later on he commanded a battalion of the Cambridgeshires at the Battle of the Somme. This battalion succeeded in capturing the Schwaben Redoubt, near Thiepval. Later on he had seen service in the battle still raging in Flanders. When he came to command the 149th Infantry Brigade at the end of September 1917 he had already won the D.S.O. and Bar. To this he subsequently added another Bar during the German offensive in March 1918. He was said to be a typical Northumbrian. A leader, gallant and war-wise, of whom Northumberland is justly proud.

When we left the line at Cherisy we had a good idea what our destination was to be. But first of all we moved a short way back in the direction of Miraumont. The 149th Infantry Brigade was quartered at Courcelles-le-Comte, a shattered village in the area vacated by the Germans after the battle on the Somme. Here we stayed for about ten days, and the battalions resumed training their men for offensive operations. One field day was particularly remarkable for a demonstration by the Air Squadron stationed at Moyenneville. We commenced operations before dawn, and I was in charge of the messages at a spot representing battle H.Q. Just before I left at the conclusion of the operations, about 9 A.M., an aeroplane swooped down over our improvised H.Q. and left a message saying 'Expect a report at B.H.Q. in an hour's time.' We returned to B.H.Q. and, sure enough, about 9.40 A.M. an aeroplane again swooped down and dropped a small packet. On opening it I was amazed to find a roll of about a dozen photographs, taken about an hour before, of the final position reached by the Infantry during the sham attack. How they managed to develop and print these photographs in the short space of time is almost a mystery. But I imagine they must have had some electrical machine for drying the negatives and prints. During this short stay out of the line I paid two visits to the old Somme battlefield. The first in company with Capt. H. Liddell, who had for some time been acting as Assistant-Brigade-Major. We rode to Grevillers and went on from there on foot to Hexham Road and Eaucourt L'Abbaye. I had visited the ground before with Lieut. Odell in June, when we were staying at Monchy-au-Bois. A good deal of salvage had been done since then, and there were fewer dead men lying about. But the scene of the fighting at Hook Sap and round the Butte of Warlencourt was still littered with helmets, rifles, and broken equipment of all sorts. Of course by this time the trenches had largely fallen in and were covered with rough rank herbage. But the wire belts and the duck-board tracks were still there. When we approached the entrance to the cellars under the ruined abbey at Eaucourt, we noticed traces of men living there. Smoke was rising out of the ruins and there were recent footmarks about, and some tins of soapy water. The story was, and I believe it was quite true, that small parties of deserters dwelt in these old deep cellars and dugouts, living on the bully beef which still covered the battlefield and on the money received for 'Souvenirs' sold at neighbouring canteens. I know of one deserter who lived there from November 1916 to June or July 1917. Apart from these slight traces of occupation, the battle-field seemed quite deserted from one end to the other.

On another occasion I went with General Riddell by car to Thiepval and we rode back through Bucquoy. This was a very interesting visit, for the General explained on the spot exactly how the Schwaben Redoubt was stormed, and how the troops were brought forward and disposed for the attack. We went over a lot of the neighbouring ground, and I was able to see how the Germans were forced out of St. Pierre Divion, Miraumont, and Beaumont Hamel. I little thought as I rode home that night through Bucquoy that I should in little more than five months' time be commanding a company in the front line in a muddy ditch outside Bucquoy. However this stay at Courcelles was invaluable later on, for it gave me a general idea of the lie of the land on the enemy side, when we were pressed back to Gommecourt and Colincamps.

We left Courcelles about October 18, and entrained at Miraumont station. We left the train near Cassel and marched to the village of Arneke, where I spent two nights at the house of the curé - a kind hospitable old man. After that we marched out of France and arrived at a camp about a mile west of Proven, in Belgium.

CHAPTER XXVI

THE HOUTHULST FOREST

I WISH I could omit all reference to the operations in Flanders 1917. Surely no one can be found to take much pride in the results of this part of the campaign. Judged by the map alone between May 1, 1917, and May 1, 1918, it will be found that we actually lost ground in Flanders, and that we were at the last hard put to it to retain any footing there at all.

It is difficult to know what motives, political or military, led to our pressing an attack with such colossal fury on this part of the line. Perhaps the Channel ports at Ostend and Zeebrugge were the prize we hoped to gain. Be that as it may, the result of our attack was to bring about a conflict of unparalleled intensity. The bulk of the English heavy artillery seemed to be concentrated on the one side and the bulk of the enemy's heavy artillery on the other. In a country like Flanders the ground is bad enough in foul weather; but where it is churned up for miles with the heaviest of shells, it becomes impossible to use tanks and next to impossible to use infantry.

Moreover, the Germans had superiority in the air. They had concentrated on aircraft the effort which we had expended on perfecting the tank. The one can be used effectively in wet weather, but the other cannot. The German had another defensive surprise for us. Owing to the nature of the ground the deep dugout was practically an impossibility. In the place, therefore, of this the German devised the concrete blockhouse or 'pill-box' as it was called. For miles behind their front line the country was dotted with pill-boxes, which could defy the tank and all but the largest kinds of shells. As soon as our operations started the rain streamed down, making conditions ten times worse for the attacking force.

All honour to those that gallantly stormed the muddy slopes of Passchendaele; to the wonderful engineers that conquered the squalid quagmires of Langemarck and Zonnebeke; to the gunners that stuck to their guns under a rain of bombs and shells, and to the transport drivers that fed them. It is a tale of wonderful gallantry and heroic endeavour. But when all is said and done, one is bound to look at the result.

On reaching the area round Proven the 50th Division was allocated to the Fifth Army (General Gough), and received orders to prepare to take part in an attack on the enemy's line between the Houthulst Forest and Passchendaele. On October 21, the day after our arrival at Proven, I went to the Fifth Army H.Q. to get all the maps and information I could relating to the new front. The Army H.Q. were in a large château north of Poperinghe, and when I got there I was received by the Colonel in charge of Intelligence with every kindness. He got me several maps, gave me the files of intelligence to glance over, and advised me to visit the Air Squadron at Proven for aeroplane photographs. He also offered to turn out a Staff car to take me back, but this kind offer I declined. My next visit was to the office of the Air Squadron, where they had a file of all photographs relating to our front. I was able to secure several useful copies, and the promise of some more. After this I returned to our camp to work on the air photos. On October 23 we marched to Proven and entrained there, getting out at Elverdinghe. A short march took us to a camp of wooden huts a little south of the château, where the 50th Division had their battle H.Q. When we arrived the huts were quite empty of all furniture; but in a short time the Brigade pioneers had made a table and forms to use in the mess. It was decided that only the General, Brigade-Major, and Signalling Officer should go forward to battle H.Q., an old German pill-box called Martin's Mill, between Widjendrift and Langemarck. The rest of the Brigade Staff were to remain at rear H.Q. at Huddersfield Dugouts on the Yser Canal close to Bard's Causeway. At this time I was much worried by what appeared to me to be an attempt to tap the information of the Brigade as to the details of the forthcoming attack. Naturally an Intelligence Officer has to be discreet at all times, but especially so at times like this. I simply record my impression although I cannot give any details.

On October 24 I went to the rear B.H.Q. at Huddersfield Dugouts. They were in the northern bank of the Yser Canal about half a mile south of Boesinghe. The front was approached by means of several long duck-board tracks, in places more like wooden bridges than the ordinary trench footboards. In the morning I did my best to investigate where these tracks started, not altogether an easy matter in an entirely strange country. In the afternoon I was asked by the Staff-Captain to see that the hot food and tea and rum for the use of the troops next morning were ready for delivery to the carrying-parties, and that the O.C. carrying-party knew exactly what to do. I found that the food &c. was ready packed up in the hot food containers by the four transport officers, but I had great difficulty in finding the officer in charge of the carrying-parties. After waiting about for over two hours I did get in touch with him. And by nightfall I had the satisfaction of seeing the hot food set off with this carrying-party up one of the tracks leading to the front. We obtained guides for this party from the 50th Divisional Signals, who gave us every assistance in their power.

The attack took place next morning about dawn, after a heavy artillery bombardment, and in the rain. Of this attack the Brigade has no need to be ashamed, although by the afternoon of the same day the remnants of its brave soldiers were withdrawn to the starting point. The 7th N.F. on the left had a shorter distance to go than the rest, but on their left flank was the Forest of Houthulst full of German snipers. On the right were the 4th N.F. and in the centre the 5th N.F.

Each battalion had to attack across a treacherous swamp, and each was confronted by a row of unbroken concrete pill-boxes, carefully concealed from aerial observation. Each battalion made ground, but each battalion was mowed down in heaps by the machine-guns in the pill-boxes. I have nothing now to give as an estimate of the casualties, except the officer casualties of the 7th N.F. Twelve officers of the 7th N.F. went over the top that morning, and one returned alive, Lieut Affleck.

The others were all killed. It gives some idea of the spirit of these gallant fellows, when I relate that Lieut Affleck was preparing a further attack on the German pill-boxes at the time he was ordered to return with the remnants of the shattered brigade. The three battalions all suffered the heaviest losses, but I have now no details except those I have given above. Lieut. Odell, the Brigade Signalling Officer, and his men did wonders in keeping the battalions in touch with B.H.Q. during the battle, and for his great personal gallantry on this occasion he received a Bar to his M.C. The shattered remnants of the battalions were drawn out of the fighting zone and given billets not far from the Yser Canal. Even here bad luck followed the 5th N.F., for a long-range shell crashed into one of the huts at Rose Camp and caused forty more casualties. In the transport lines on the west side of the Yser Canal Capt. Neville, the Q.M. of the 7th N.F., was killed by a bomb next day. An old soldier with a wonderful record of service, he had preferred to stick to his battalion instead of taking promotion. I have already called him the prince of quarter masters. I had also to lament him as a very kind and generous friend.

We now received orders to retire to the rest area about Ondank, and on October 26 I was sent to take over a camp for B.H.Q. On the way I called at D.H.Q. at Elverdinghe Château, where I was very courteously received by the 'Q' Staff - Col. Cartwright and Major McCracken - who made many sympathetic inquiries after the officers in the Brigade.

We were now quartered in some old wooden huts, possibly constructed by the French; and though very comfortable inside they were hardly bomb-proof. At nights all the back areas round Ypres were heavily bombed and a lot of horses were killed every night and a certain number of men as well.

On October 27 the poor shattered remnants of my battalion passed B.H.Q., very weary and very few in numbers. Besides the Battalion H.Q. Company there were just enough men to make one decent-sized company. Lieut.-Col. G. Scott Jackson stopped to speak to me, and the tears trickled down his weather-beaten face, as he said 'Buckley, this has fairly done me.' Only those who have had a fine battalion cut to pieces can realise the feelings of their commander at such a moment.

I set to work with my observers packing a wall of sandbags round the wooden huts, as a protection against bomb splinters. It was not possible to protect the roof, but these sandbags were effective against anything but a direct hit.

I have never known German night bombing more persistent or more heavy than it was in the Salient just at this time. And although we never got a bomb in the same field as our camp they dropped close enough to be disturbing. A camp with some of the Divisional details was struck some little way from us, and the same night D.H.Q. at Elverdinghe Château were bombed, several motor-lorries being set on fire.

It was too far back for us to be troubled with much shelling, and the German long-range guns fired mostly over our heads at the more attractive targets of Poperinghe and Proven. One day during this short rest, October 29, I had a ride round with Lieut. Odell in search of a field-cashier's office where money could be drawn to pay Brigade details. After a long ride to different places we landed up at a Canadian Cashier's Office near Poperinghe; at this time the Canadians were on Passchendaele Ridge. About November 5 the Brigade returned to the line for a few days before the Division was taken out. On that day I returned with the Staff-Captain and Capt. G. Bell (6th N.F., Assistant-Staff-Captain) to Huddersfield Dugouts. On the following day I walked nearly as far as the Steenbeke at Martin's Mill, and the ground around Langemarck was about as dreary and shattered as any that I have ever seen. It was well described to me once as 'utter squalor.' Next day I went to the camp of the 4th N.F. south of Langemarck and to Marsouine camp, to arrange certain details of the relief. The same night the Brigade was relieved, but I was left in charge at Huddersfield Dugouts till the evening of November 8 when I returned to the camp at Ondank. On November 12 the Brigade entrained at Elverdinghe station and were taken through St. Omer to Watten station. We marched from there in the dark to the little village of Serques. We were now to have about a month's rest and training before returning again to the Salient.

CHAPTER XXVII

DIVISIONAL REST NEAR ST. OMER

SERQUES WAS QUITE a pleasant little village to stay at, but the arrangements for training were very scanty. I had to search round for suitable spots for rifle-ranges, and to agree with the owners for suitable compensation. Also I had to make some of the arrangements for a ferry boat to convey the troops across the Canal De L'Aa to a good training-ground between Watten and St. Momelin. On November 14 I paid my first visit to St. Omer, which is a nice town with plenty of good shops.

Lieut.-Col. G.R.B. Spain, C.M.G., of the 6th N.F. came to command the Brigade during the absence of Brigadier-General Riddell on leave. He was a man of remarkable erudition and a collector of prints and other things. And I soon found that we had many things in common and many interesting talks I had with him on a variety of subjects.

We discovered together several early flint implements and arrow-heads about Serques, and he told me a lot about the early Stone Age, which interested me greatly and set me looking for these interesting relics wherever we happened to be quartered.[15] Shortly after this time Lieut.-Col. Scott Jackson left the 7th N.F. to join the R.A.M.C. and to take command of a base hospital. He was succeeded by Capt. H. Liddell, M.C., who now became Lieut.-Col. in command of the battalion.

After staying at Serques for about two weeks the Brigade moved to the area around Tournehem. This was not such a flat watery country; and we had better quarters in the house of the curé of the place.

15. At Coigneux I found a series of early implements in which the British Museum took considerable interest.

It was decided to hold Brigade Sports here, and I was sent off to Boulogne to buy the prizes. I went there and back in a Divisional Staff car. I had lunch at the Officers' Club, where the W.A.A.C.'s were serving as waitresses; and very nice it was to see their fresh English faces again. A visit to Boulogne when you are not going on leave brings back rather melancholy feelings, and I was glad to leave the place.

An incident happened at Nortleulinghem, which was rather unfortunate for it spoilt an unbroken record. The 7th N.F., who were stationed at this place, were ordered to provide a field-firing demonstration for the Divisional Staff. The demonstration was to include the firing of a number of smoke-bombs - rifle-grenades with a small can of phosphorus at the end. Their successful discharge required considerable practice and nerve.

As Lieut. H. Richardson, the Bombing Officer of the 7th N.F., was away I was asked to come over and instruct the men how to fire these new weapons off. There were only two mornings in which to instruct them before the demonstration came off. Of course it was a very hurried proceeding, and I was rather horrified to find that the men knew practically nothing about rifle-grenades. (Most of the trained rifle-bombers had become casualties in the battle at Houthulst.) I did what I could to explain the working of the smoke rifle-bomb; but on the first practice taking place one of the men succeeded in blowing off the forefinger of another man, through firing too soon. Of course that was not a fatal accident, but it put the man out of action for the rest of the war - my only serious accident in bombing of any kind. When the demonstration came off, there were to my great relief no further regrettable incidents of that sort.

On December 9 we began to prepare to return to the Salient, and I went with certain advanced details to Watten, where I spent the night in one of the houses. I managed to get a very passable dinner at the best local inn. We entrained next day at Watten station and were taken by rail to Brandhoek; marching to a camp quite close to the station.

I had seen in some of our Intelligence papers that the 14th Division was in a Corps immediately on our left, and I therefore knew that I might have a chance of getting in touch with my brother George. Accordingly I walked to Vlamertinghe next day and heard that his battalion was stationed in a camp at St. Jean. On December 12 I was sent forward to take over B.H.Q. in Ypres, at a convent at the N.E. corner of the city. The higher floors of the convent were all in ruins, but the ground floors were more or less intact, and in these we had our rooms and offices. The mess room was under a pile of rubbish outside. Having made the arrangements with the 150th Infantry Brigade, whom we were relieving, I had still an hour to spare before B.H.Q. would arrive. So I decided to walk over to St. Jean and inquire for my brother's battalion. It took me about twenty minutes to get there, but there was no difficulty in finding the battalion or their H.Q. So I marched up to the H.Q. hut and asked to see Capt. Buckley. He came out at once and was very surprised to see me, for he had no idea where I was at this time. It was a hurried but exceedingly pleasant meeting. I had only twenty minutes to spare, and he was just going forward to the front line that night. So we had to 'swop yarns' very quickly. And he walked back part of the way with me towards Ypres. I thought he looked very worn out and depressed. He had had a very hard time in the Salient, and in a few days he was back in hospital with influenza.

CHAPTER XXVIII

THE PASSCHENDAELE RIDGE

THE 50TH DIVISION were holding the line in front of Passchendaele Village and a little to the south. On our right were the West Riding Territorials, the 49th Division, commanded by Major-General Cameron (once one of our brigadiers); on the left the 14th Division. Only one brigade was in the line at a time - another remaining in support around Ypres and the other back at rest about Brandhoek. Thus a brigade went to close support for four days, to the front line for four days, and then back to the rest area for four days. This seems to be an easy method of holding the line; but, owing to the nature of the ground and to the heavy shelling that went on most of the day and night in the forward areas, it was impossible to keep a brigade very long in the front line. The battle on the ridge had been over for some time, but neither side was yet prepared to disperse its heavy concentration of guns. But the heavy firing was gradually, very gradually, becoming less severe.

Ypres itself had been badly knocked about during the great battle. Most of the troops billeted in Ypres lived underground, but whilst I was living there it was never severely shelled. Shrapnel was fired occasionally at the balloons over the city, and also about the Menin Gate and the roads leading towards the east end of the city. But there were no heavy guns in Ypres itself, and there was at present no particular reason for shelling it. We therefore had not an unpleasant time ourselves in the city. I believe that the H.Q. at the convent were shelled whilst we were in the front line, but that only happened once.

On December 13 I went for a walk of inspection as far as Dan Cottages, some old German pill-boxes, where the forward brigade had their H.Q. For the first mile or so from Ypres the ground seemed to be recovering from the heavy shelling it had received, and there was a good deal of grass now growing about the old British front line trenches. But as you got farther forward to the area of the heavy guns, the ground was badly shattered and every shell-hole full of water. Between this point and B.H.Q. the conditions were simply awful. A vast swamp of yellow-brown mud divided into craters of large size - all full of watery slime. And so it went on as far as the eye could see.

Here and there there were oases of dry ground, generally holding several heavy guns and dumps of ammunition. Whilst at intervals the swamp was intersected by a wooden road, used by the lorries to bring up ammunition, and by two or three duck-board tracks which ran winding through the awful mess of mud and water. These tracks were supported on wooden piles driven into the mud, and were more like wooden bridges than tracks. Sometimes they rested on firm ground, but mostly they were held up in the air by the wooden piles. Again right through the devastated area ran a good paved road from Ypres towards Zonnebeke. Here and there in some of the drier spots you could see queer white mounds - the concrete pill-boxes, some of which were still sound enough, but others broken in and waterlogged. The pill-boxes and the road and the wooden tracks were of course well known to the German artillery, who lavished a great deal of ammunition every day on each of these targets. But owing to the methodical way in which the Germans fired on the tracks, it was always possible to mend them wherever they were smashed. Between 2 A.M. and 8 A.M. practically no shells came over on to the tracks, and during this time each day gangs of men went out and mended the damage done to them.

When the frost came and solidified the mud, travelling became safer if not so easy; for it was then possible to leave the tracks and go across country by walking round the edges of the shell craters. All along the road there was ceaseless activity day and night. Lines and lines of lorries going backwards or forwards, limbers, wagons, men. When the enemy shelled the road, generally some damage was done, and it was not uncommon to see pools of blood in the road and the litter of broken vehicles. At intervals along the road there were vast dumps of ammunition and stores, and on the side tracks huge piles of every sort of salvage.

Forward again of B.H.Q. the country was perhaps not so badly smashed, except in the spots most exposed to shell fire. But the shell-holes were often full of German dead - I counted nearly 100 within a quarter of a mile of Dan Cottages. And on the forward wooden tracks used by our transport, the ground reeked like a slaughter-house. Fragments of everything just swept off the tracks. The limbs and bodies of the pack-mules lying sometimes in heaps sometimes at intervals all along the route. Of course the nearer you approached to Passchendaele Ridge the drier and firmer was the ground. But that awful swamp behind has probably no parallel in the history of war. How the Engineers overcame it is really a marvel. And great credit indeed must be given to this very efficient branch of the Army, and to the men who laboured there under the terrible conditions around them. I have mentioned the German dead; there was no doubt little time to give to them. But I hardly saw one body of a British soldier who had been left without burial.

On December 15 I went with General Riddell to visit the 5th N.F. Battalion H.Q. at Tyne Cottages, some pill-boxes about half-way between forward B.H.Q. and Passchendaele. It was a long walk, and we went up the Zonnebeke Road till we were in the neighbourhood of that village, then along the mule track to Tyne Cottages. Whilst we were talking with Major A. Irwin at the pill-box a few light shells came over and sprinkled us with earth. It was best to be either inside or well away from a pill-box: but as the entrance to this pill-box was like a rabbit-hole and close to the ground General Riddell preferred to stand outside. After that we paid a visit to Dan Cottages, and returned back along the wooden tracks to Ypres.

Next day B.H.Q. went forward to Dan Cottages and stayed there for four days. The Brigade observers were employed in two ways, partly as observers and partly as a gas guard for the B.H.Q. pill-box. This pill-box had already stood one or two strong blows from shells, but it still appeared to be pretty sound. The door of course faced the enemy, but was protected by a stout concrete wall and a bank of earth outside that.

It will be seen from the above plan that the quarters were very confined - the bunks being roughly six feet long and the room rather over six feet high.

One observer stood in the narrow passage outside the door as sentry and gas guard. He was of course relieved every four hours, and at night there were generally two on duty. The other observers who were not on this duty held a post about Hillside Farm about a mile forward of Dan Cottages. This was not altogether a healthy spot, but a good view was obtained towards Moorslede.

In this area observers were asked to pay special attention to the enemy's shelling, noticing the direction from which the sound of the firing came and the areas shelled and approximately the number of rounds. I had of course to write out the Brigade Intelligence Report each morning. The last night we were in these quarters a number of gas-shells were fired round the batteries and B.H.Q. They made the atmosphere very unpleasant; and though they were not thick enough to necessitate wearing the respirator, I suffered, especially the following night, from their effects.

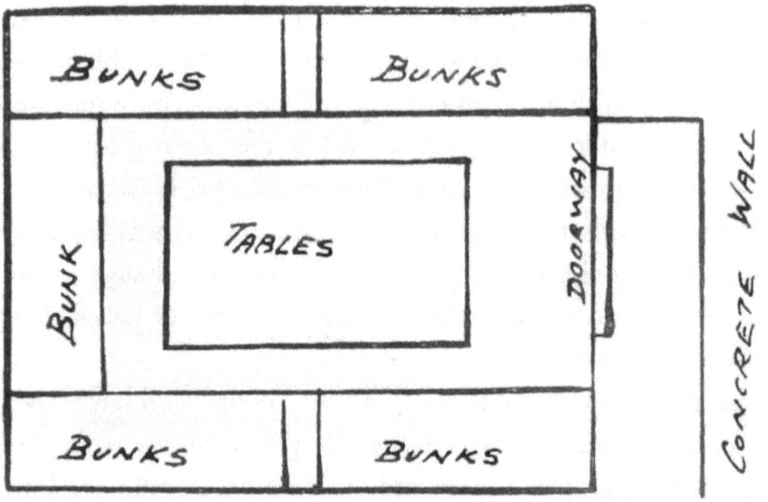

Plan of B.H.Q. (Judah House), Dan Cottages.

On December 20 we were relieved and moved back to the rest area at Brandhoek, where we were glad to have four days' rest. On Christmas Eve we moved to our old quarters at Ypres, and the following night we had an excellent Christmas dinner thanks to the good services of Lieut. Behrens, our French interpreter, an old machine-gunner of Verdun. On December 28 we again went to the front area and held the line for four days. It was always the custom for one of the officers of the Brigade to keep awake on duty during part of the night. We took it in turns and did two-hour shifts. On the morning of December 31 it happened to be my turn to be awake on duty just about dawn. And this saved me from a very rude awakening. That morning the enemy had decided on a bombardment of our Divisional front and he commenced proceedings by shelling Dan Cottages with a battery of 4-inch naval guns, a very accurate weapon. We got a shell on the roof of the pill-box which gave a nasty concussion and put all the lights out. That woke the rest of the Staff up except the Artillery Officer. I had hardly got the lights on again when we got another shell on the roof. Again the lights went out, and this time a piece of concrete fell out of the roof and crashed on to the floor, knocking over some of our belongings, but fortunately missing the officers inside.

A few small fragments of concrete also dropped on the face of the Artillery Liaison Officer who had slept peacefully through the first concussion. He woke up then with a comical look of surprise, as if some one were playing a joke on him. Although another shell struck the bank at the doorway we had no more on the roof, and no casualties - only we found that all our telephone wires had been cut. I wonder whether our roof would have stood another direct hit! Later on in the day I filled the holes in the roof outside with blocks of ice and frozen earth, in fact anything I could find to act as a 'burster' in case of further shelling. At 12 o'clock midnight, being the beginning of New Year's Day, our artillery fired their usual reminder at the enemy. It has been a point of honour with us to fire off all our guns as soon as possible after the New Year came in. On the evening of January 1 we were relieved and moved back to Brandhoek. On January 3 the Division was taken farther back for a rest, and the Brigade marched to the district about Watou on the French border.

Having served for two years abroad I applied for a month's leave - it was a privilege granted to Staff Officers who needed a rest. My leave warrant reached me on January 5, and next day I left Watou and entrained at Poperinghe for Boulogne.

CHAPTER XXIX

GOOD-BYE TO THE 50TH DIVISION

WHEN I RETURNED to Ypres on February 8, 1918, I found that some very drastic changes had taken place in the grouping of battalions. Instead of four battalions to a brigade, there were now to be three; and every division was to be provided with a Pioneer battalion. This meant that the 50th Division, who already possessed a battalion of pioneers, had to part with a battalion from each brigade. And these battalions would have to be attached as pioneer battalions to other divisions who possessed no pioneer battalion. As the junior battalion in the Northumberlands, the 7th N.F. were selected to go from the 149th Infantry Brigade; and their companions in misfortune were the 9th D.L.I. and the 5th Border Regiment. Major-General Sir P.S. Wilkinson, K.C.M.G., our Divisional Commander, was good enough to say that he was parting with three of his best battalions.

Although I had been attached to the Staff of the 149th Infantry Brigade since May 1916 I was included in the General Order that all detached officers should join their respective battalions before they left the Division. At the time this looked very hard. I had been a specialist for over two years and had got completely out of touch with company work. But I have no doubt now that in the events which happened I was very lucky to leave the 50th Division at this juncture. In six weeks' time I was, through the good offices of the Battalion H.Q., given an Intelligence job with our new Division; and the experience I had gained with the 50th Division was not wasted as I had feared it might be. Also there went with me from the 149th Infantry Brigade four highly-trained observers who formed the nucleus and backbone of the 42nd Divisional observers. On returning to the 7th N.F. I lost my acting-captaincy and became second in command to C Company. Also I had to part with many good friends in the old Brigade: some of them I was destined never to meet again. Lieut. E.W. Styles who was attached to the 149th Trench-Mortar Battery was unhappily killed during the German offensive; a great friend whom I shall always miss. My bombing orderly, L.-C. Fairclough, was also killed during the same operations.

When I joined the 7th N.F. they were stationed at St. Jean - in Alnwick Camp. And here the battalion said good-bye to the Brigade.

It was a singular turn of fate that this should occur here. The 7th N.F. had fought their first battle with the Brigade on this spot in April 1915, and the name of the camp was of course taken from the town where their H.Q. were stationed at home. When he came to say farewell to the battalion, General Riddell referred to this curious coincidence and also bade us remember the regimental motto 'Quo Fata Vocant' ('Whither the Fates call'). So we left the Ypres Salient for the last time. And although I went into Belgium again with the Army of Occupation, I have never set foot in Flanders again. Of all countries on earth it is surely the most dismal and unhappy. At least so it appeared to me.

CHAPTER XXX

DIGGING TRENCHES ABOUT LOOS

BEFORE WE LEFT the 50th Division we learnt that we were to join the 42nd (East Lancashire) Territorial Division, commanded at this time by Major-General A. Solly-Flood, C.M.G., D.S.O. The latter Division had seen service in Egypt and Gallipoli before coming to France, and they were now resting in the Bethune area, having just left the trenches between Cambrin and Loos. This was in the I Corps area of the First Army. As pioneers to the 42nd Division the 7th N.F. became Divisional troops, directly under the command of the Divisional Staff and no longer in a brigade. The three brigades of our new division were the 125th (Lancs. Fusiliers), 126th (East Lancashire), and 127th (Manchester) - all Territorial brigades. The Staff of the 42nd Division treated their new pioneer battalion with kindness and consideration; and I believe we were called on occasion 'Solly-Flood's Pets.' On the other hand there was friction at times between the men of the 42nd Division and the men of the 7th N.F.

The whole Division had hitherto been drawn from the East Lancashire area - Manchester, Oldham, Bury, &c., and they looked upon us rather as intruders. The Northumberlands were of course not the people to let slip so admirable an opportunity of accepting a feud: and in October 1918 they committed the unforgivable sin of winning the Divisional Association Football Cup, which completed their unpopularity.

And for a battalion which had seen the hard service of the 7th N.F., the stock jests generally levelled at a pioneer battalion were a little out of place. The 42nd Division proved themselves a hard fighting division in 1918, and lived up to their motto 'Go one better.'

The 7th N.F. left the Ypres area about February 11, 1918, and after spending a few days at Brandhock they were conveyed in motor-buses to the small village of Fouquereuil, west of Bethune.

Here the battalion was instructed to help the pioneers of the 6th Division, who were holding the front line trenches between Cambrin and Loos. Accordingly three companies of the 7th N.F. were detached from the battalion and sent to the forward area. I went with C Company (Capt. Herriott) to Philosophe, a small colliery village still partly inhabited by civilians, though fairly close to the front line.

Our daily work was making reserve defences, trenches, deep dugouts, and machine-gun emplacements between Vermelles and Loos. During our stay of about a week at Philosophe the village was quiet. But one night the enemy's guns sent a perfect stream of shells just over the tops of the cottages for about twenty minutes. About a week after we left the village it was completely knocked to bits by the enemy's 10-inch howitzer shells.

Our next visit was to some reserve trenches at Cambrin, where we stayed for about a week, improving the defences. It was a quiet, easy time, though not far behind the front line. After this the four companies of the 7th N.F. were reduced to three, and I was transferred to A Company at Sailly-Labourse. Here we were some distance behind the front line, but working-parties were taken up to the forward area, and I used to go and inspect them. Shortly after our arrival at Sailly the enemy began to shell the back areas, causing great annoyance and some casualties to the civilian population, generally to children. They had been allowed to live here many months in peace, although not five miles away from the enemy's trenches. Even Sailly-Labourse received almost daily salvoes from long-range guns.

I had a very unpleasant experience myself in my billet, a brick cottage, one night about March 12. I was in bed on the first floor - the only person in the cottage except monsieur and madame who slept in the cellar. About midnight the enemy's 4-inch naval guns started shelling the place. Three shells in succession passed just over the roof of my cottage, one smashed the next house to pieces; the next fell into our little back garden, eight yards from the cottage; and the third struck the road on the other side. After that I got up and joined monsieur and madame for ten minutes in the cellar, until the shelling had ceased. Then back to bed. But next day I took the precaution of changing my billet - going to the cellar of the broken house next door.

It was a piteous sight to see the poor French folk as they fled from their homes, with their most cherished belongings packed on to small carts.

About this time the 42nd Division decided to form a party of observers, known as 'Divisional Observers,' who were intended to keep a watch on the enemy during a battle and to report all sudden movements to the Division. They were really intended to collect information for D.H.Q. at times when the ordinary avenues of information had broken down. At first the party consisted of one officer and nine trained observers: but later on it was increased by the inclusion of signallers and one or two additional men.

On March 15, 1918, I was instructed to return to Lapugnoy to Battalion H.Q. in order to organise and command this new party of men. I obtained this job through the kind recommendation of the Colonel and Adjutant of the 7th N.F. Although this side of Intelligence was not perhaps the one that I had most experience of, yet I hailed my return to an Intelligence job with delight.

When I reached Lapugnoy no observers had yet arrived, but next day I went to interview Capt. E.C.B. Kirsopp, M.C., the G.S.O. III, who was the officer on the Staff directly responsible for the equipment and movements of the observers. Capt. Kirsopp was, I believe, the father of the observers, i.e. responsible for their formation, and he showed at all times an interest and a kindness which were fully appreciated. His faith in the possibilities of the party never wavered, although for some time it was difficult to know how to make their information quick and effective. However, he never lost hope in us, and he never ceased to try to improve the means of communication between the observers and D.H.Q. Amongst other things he got for the observers two very powerful telescopes, with a magnification of forty-five times. And although these glasses could not, owing to their size and the weight of their fittings, be used during the moving warfare, at a later stage they proved simply invaluable for making target sketches of the enemy's defences. Another officer who did us good service was Lieut. C.R. Stride, the Q.M. of the 7th N.F. Without his aid the heavy telescopes would never have gone into action, and the observers would often have been without rations. He always took an interest in the little party, and provided us with many welcome comforts from his store.[16]

On March 19 the following observers reported to me. From the 7th N.F. L.-C. J. Cowen and Ptes. J. King, W. Fail, and R. Ewart - all of whom were old friends and observers of the 149th Infantry Brigade; from the 125th Infantry Brigade L.-C. J. Flynn; from the 126th Infantry Brigade Ptes. F. Dunkerley and F. Turner; from the 127th Infantry Brigade Corp. Walker and Pte. A. Morris. Owing to casualties and to the observers being recalled to their battalions the personnel of the party was always changing. But of the above, the four men of the 7th N.F. and Pte. F. Turner practically remained with the observers from first to last.

For about a week I stayed at Lapugnoy, giving lectures to the observers and carrying out some field training with the compass and protractor. But our peaceful existence in the back area was not destined to last long. On Friday, March 22, I was instructed to take the observers to the 42nd Division Signal School at Bethune, in order that the men might go through a course of signalling. We reached the Signal School at 4 P.M. on Friday, and at 10 P.M. the same night, we received orders that all officers and men at the school were to be ready to move at 6 A.M. next morning. The long expected blow had fallen at last. The enemy had already launched the first wave of his great offensive.

16. Lieut.-Col. H. Liddell, D.S.O., M.C., was most generous in providing men to replace casualties and in sending us four signallers from the 7th N.F. H.Q.

CHAPTER XXXI

THE GERMAN OFFENSIVE 1918 - SECOND BATTLE OF ARRAS

MARCH 23, 1918 was a fine day: and that was lucky for us, for we had a long day in the open before us. We got a hurried breakfast about six o'clock, and were soon marching by road to the place of assembly on the road from Bethune to Hesdigneul. Here we had a wait of several hours on the roadside, whilst an unending stream of motor-buses hurried past all going southwards. It was rumoured that our destination was Basseux, five miles S.W. of Arras; and I hoped it was true, for I knew the district better than any other in France. At last the buses allotted to the Divisional troops drew up and we got aboard and set off on our journey to the south. We went through Labuissière to St. Pol, and thence through Frévent to Doullens, and then north-east along the road towards Arras. Except for a few large and recent shell-holes by the roadside we saw little unusual until we began to get near Arras. We stopped for a few minutes near the C.C.S. at Laherlière, and I got off and asked one of the hospital orderlies how things were going on. We were told that our fellows had had a bad day on the 22nd, but that to-day far fewer casualties had passed through the station. Soon after that we met a number of French civilians with carts streaming back from Arras, guarded by French soldiers. We knew then that things were not going too well in front.

When we reached Basseux about 6 P.M. the buses were turned round and we went on in an easterly direction till we reached Ayette.

Here we got down and marched in the darkness to the ruined village of Adinfer. Continual flashes in the direction of Monchy-le-Preux and an intermittent roar from our long-range guns near at hand showed that fighting was still going on. But no shells arrived to add to our discomfort. The observers had to bivouac in Adinfer Wood, a cheerless proceeding after our long journey down, for we had no blankets and no chance of getting a hot meal. Some artillerymen gave me a drink of water, which I remember with gratitude, for I had had no chance of a drink since 6 A.M., and the roads had been choked with dust. There was a keen frost that night, and I could not sleep for long. When daylight came I managed to light a small fire and to heat up a tin of 'Machonchie'; and this put a little more life into me. After that I went to Adinfer where the Divisional Staff were quartered in wooden huts. Here I got a cup of coffee and had a chat with the Divisional Intelligence Officer, Lieut. G.F. Doble, M.C. I found that D.H.Q. were moving back to Monchy-au-Bois. My instructions were to reconnoitre the roads from Ayette towards Bucquoy, Ablainzevelle, and Courcelles-le-Comte. So after getting quarters for my party at a ruined cottage in the wood, I set out with most of my men and spent the whole afternoon tramping the roads as far as Ablainzevelle and back again towards Moyenneville. Unfortunately as events proved this was time and labour lost. For when I reported to Capt. Kirsopp at Monchy-au-Bois I found that the 42nd Division had received orders from the IV Corps to hold the line farther south, towards Behagnies and Sapignies. D.H.Q. were to move next day to a camp between Logeast Wood and Bucquoy. I was told to send a party of observers to the east end of Logeast Wood and to pay a visit myself to the H.Q. near Bucquoy. The night was again spent in Adinfer Wood; but it was more comfortable for we had collected some rations and blankets and were less exposed to the weather.

Next morning (March 25) I moved across country with L.-C. Flynn to the camp between Logeast Wood and Bucquoy. The country-side seemed deserted and no sound of firing could be heard. L.-C. Cowen took two observers to the east end of Logeast Wood and spent the day there, but nothing of importance could be seen. They were, however, shelled by the enemy for a time in the afternoon. Later on in the day there were more signs of the enemy's activity. A large dump exploded at Courcelles, but it may have been done by our own R.E.'s. And it was reported that the Germans were advancing towards Achiet-le-Grand. I found out that evening that D.H.Q. had moved back to the village of Fonquevillers; so I decided to move my men more in that direction; and after nightfall the observers marched along the road through Monchy-au-Bois to Bienvillers.

On this road we saw guns and transport in large numbers, mostly going south. It was fairly evident to my mind that the enemy had made another advance during the day, but definite news was hard to get. Hundreds of shells from the German 4-inch naval guns fell about the roads all night, but I heard not one of them explode. They must have been a rotten lot of ammunition. On arriving at Bienvillers the observers got a billet in the cellars of a shattered house at the north end of the village. A little later I went to Fonquevillers to get news from D.H.Q. - and instructions for next day. The Divisional Staff were quartered in some Nissen huts. When I arrived they had no particular news, but I was asked to send a post of observers again, if possible, to the east end of Logeast Wood, which was thought to be still in our hands. After this I returned to Bienvillers about midnight and arranged for an early start next day.

In the morning (March 26) we were cooking tea and bacon about 3.45 A.M. when a very tired and draggled officer came in. He said he had just ridden over from Bapaume on a motor-cycle and he told us a sorry tale. He evidently thought that the Germans had broken right through on the Fifth Army front (i.e. on our right), and that the British forces were about to be surrounded. Bapaume was on fire, and the British Army defeated and broken in the south. This was the first definite news I had of the misfortunes in the Somme area. It was disquieting enough and I determined to approach Logeast Wood with caution and to keep a sharp look-out for unusual movement as we went forward. Accompanied by Ptes. Fail and Ewart I went across country towards Bucquoy as the light was beginning to break. We noticed that the large trees on the road to Hannescamps had been prepared by the R.E.'s for felling with gun cotton - the charges being ready and tied to the trunks so as to throw them across the road. The roads were already full, mostly horse transport pouring rapidly through Bienvillers towards Souastre. Transport from the south-east coming in our direction through Hannescamps appeared to be in a panic and expecting pursuit by the German cavalry. Once we got away from the road and reached Le Quesnoy Farm there was little movement to be seen. A few small parties of our men moving towards us across the open and here and there a limber. Nothing in a hurry, nothing at all to indicate a retreat on our own front, though it was actually taking place at the time. There was no sound of firing, and no shells. A battery of field guns still lay in a hollow just west of Bucquoy, and this sight rather reassured me; so I decided to push on a bit. Leaving my two observers on the ridge west of Dierville Farm I approached the ruined buildings of the farm which lie a little west of the road between Bucquoy and Ayette. While I was here I saw some of our infantry marching along this road out of Bucquoy and forming a line along it. One of them asked me where they could get in touch with our troops on the left. Though I had been told to expect them east of Logeast Wood they had in fact fallen back during the night and were even now about to leave Ablainzevelle. The troops I saw on the road were in fact taking up a line of resistance, for they were the British front line. After this I decided that Dierville Farm could be held as an O.P. for the time being; and so sending my two observers on, I returned to Bienvillers to get a little much needed rest. As I went back there was still no shelling and no sound of rifle fire. Yet it afterwards transpired that the enemy had already pushed his outposts forward into Ablainzevelle and west of Logeast Wood. Surely it was on this part of the front one of the most silent advances made in the war. When they returned my observers reported all quiet at Dierville Farm, but the two observers that relieved them at 10 A.M. found the enemy guns more active. After midday a number of shells were sent into the village of Bucquoy and not far from the farm.

When I got back the roads through Bienvillers became more crowded than ever with horse transport, and many guns were being moved on the road from Monchy-au-Bois. The sides of the road, too, became crowded with infantry, who were apparently awaiting orders to move forward. In spite of the congestion on the roads the enemy made only one attempt that day to harass them. A 10-inch shell from a long-range gun fell in an open field about 100 yards short of Bienvillers Church, but it did no damage except to the field. The stream of traffic through the village continued without ceasing all that day. At 4 P.M. I received orders from the Division to join the 7th N.F. near Essarts and to come under the command of the O.C. 7th N.F. It was found impossible to make any direct use of the observers at the time owing to the disorganisation and uncertainty that prevailed; so they were added temporarily as a reinforcement to the battalion. It was indeed a crisis in the fate of the right wing of the Third Army, though at the time we did not realise it. At 6 P.M. the observers left Bienvillers and went forward along the road to Hannescamps, meeting many wounded on the road and a few other parties of troops returning. We found the battalion in a hollow west of Essarts. They were just preparing to move. On reporting to Major McLeod, who was in temporary command of the battalion, I was told to attach the observers to the H.Q. Company.

The battalion had already had a brush with the enemy. On the preceding day, March 25, about midday they had advanced in artillery formation from Logeast Wood towards Achiet-le-Grand.

Near that village they had come under direct fire from the enemy's field artillery and they had been shelled also with 5.9-inch howitzers. One company suffered rather severe casualties, but the battalion succeeded in passing through the village and filling a gap in the line. Later on in the day they had been relieved by the neighbouring Brigade and received orders to fall back first to Logeast Wood and later on to Ablainzevelle. The latter place they were ordered to leave at 8 A.M. that morning. Eventually they reached the place where I found them. The men were all in good spirits and evidently pleased with their part in the rearguard action. Very soon after I joined them the battalion was moved again, this time about a quarter of a mile to the south across the Bucquoy-Bienvillers Road. Here we waited till further orders should arrive, and meantime some hot soup and rum were served out. Then we all lay down in the open, with blankets it is true, but the air was so frosty that little sleep was possible. About midnight we got orders to go to some trenches just east of the village of Essarts. We marched forward to this place, about a mile, without any interference from the enemy. H.Q. were established in a small tin hut in the village. Although there were still many trees about the place, all trace of the buildings had disappeared except one or two cellars and some piles of rubbish. We found our field batteries stationed quite close to us, to the west and north of Essarts, and one in a small hollow to the east. These batteries kept up a pretty constant fire during the night; but so far the enemy did not reply. All our heavy guns seem to have been taken away, except possibly one battery of 60-pounder guns near Hannescamps.

The two following days, March 27 and 28, were memorable for a continuous series of attacks by the enemy along the whole of our front.

On the morning of the 27th I went to the east side of the Essarts Wood to note what was going on, and I sent a party of observers farther north to the high ground at Le Quesnoy Farm. About 10.30 A.M. the enemy's artillery opened a scattered fire on the neighbourhood of Essarts, apparently searching the hollows for our battery positions. But it was not until 11 A.M. that the enemy started to shell our forward positions. From 11 A.M. to 11.25 A.M. a heavy barrage of flame-shells was put down about Dierville Farm and along the road leading from Bucquoy to Ayette. I am told that they did not do much damage, but they were certainly a terrible sight. The flames that burst from these shells when they reached the ground rose up thirty or forty feet in the air, flared on for a few moments, and then disappeared into a dirty black smoke. For twenty-five minutes they came over fast, and they did not finally cease till 11.45 A.M. At the same time Biez Wood on our right was heavily shelled and the area to the south of Bucquoy. Our field batteries at Essarts made a gallant reply, pouring in an unceasing rain of shrapnel wherever the enemy was suspected to be concentrating. This in turn drew a very unpleasant fire on to Essarts, which went on without break till 2 P.M. After that the enemy's counter-battery guns must have run out of ammunition, for they gave little more trouble for the rest of the day. Our field guns however continued to fire all that day and through the greater part of the night; their fire did not slacken whether shells were bursting around them or not. And great credit must be given to these gunners for their share in dispersing five enemy attacks. The battery on the east side of the wood, belonging to the 41st Division, came in for some very severe shelling, but the gunners never ceased to fire or to carry ammunition forward to the guns in full view of the enemy. As things had become rather hot around our tin hut, H.Q. were moved to a cellar, used as a dressing-station, where the doctor, Capt. C.F. Lidderdale, made room for us.

During the evening the battalion got orders to be prepared to form a defensive flank between Le Quesnoy Farm and Adinfer Wood. The enemy's attacks had made progress on our left towards Ayette, and it was feared that he might break through in that direction. Next morning, however, March 28, still found us at Essarts. The battalion was ordered to leave the trenches and to fall back behind the line of batteries on the west of the wood. In order to get a view of what was going on in front, I was sent by the Adjutant with two observers[17] to a point east of the wood, and we dug ourselves in in some partly-formed trenches there. In these trenches we stayed till well on into the afternoon, sending in reports every half-hour of what we could see to the H.Q. of the Infantry Brigade in Essarts. Evidently the enemy had renewed his attacks, for there was heavy shelling all along the front, and a number of shells again came in amongst the batteries about Essarts. During the afternoon the 7th N.F. moved forward to some trenches in support, on the ridge east of Essarts. And there the observers joined them after dark. The firing had been hot all day, but it now died down. And it really looked as if the enemy's attacks had become exhausted for the time being.

17. Ptes. Fail and Ewart.

This forward move by the battalion was, I found, preliminary to taking over the front line trenches to the north and east of Bucquoy. And shortly before midnight we moved out through the darkness and took over these trenches.[18] The front line lay on the high ground beyond the village. The H.Q. which we took over were in a mined dugout to the west of the village. This dugout had been made by the Germans before the end of 1916, and it was small but very deep. It soon became unconscionably stuffy, as there was only one entrance. But it was better than being in the open.

Next day the enemy kept fairly quiet, but the village was shelled occasionally with heavy howitzers. I went out with two observers to the high ground west of Dierville Farm. But we saw no movement by the enemy's troops. Later on the enemy's guns became more active on the roads, and the road leading back to Essarts received salvoes all day. Orders came for our relief which was to start after dark. It was not until 10 P.M. that the companies in the front line were relieved and the H.Q. Company was free to move off. The journey to Fonquevillers, where we were going, was not without interference from the enemy. Hitherto I had had great luck in escaping being shelled on the roads at night, but to-night my luck was out. As we moved back along the road to Essarts - the doctor and I at the end of the column - a number of gas-shells were dropped on the windward side of the road. They were not thick enough to stop us, but they smelt very bad. As we approached the cross-roads east of Essarts a 5.9-inch shell fell close by the roadside. We had a shower of mud thrown over us by this shell, and three more came in quick succession, but not quite so unpleasantly close.

An incident also of a disagreeable kind occurred near the end of our journey. Between Gommecourt and Fonquevillers we had to halt, until the trenches allotted to us had been located. At this point the road was packed with troops returning from the line; and some battalions brought their cookers here, so that the road was crammed almost tight with

18. Major V. Merivale, M.C. (C Company), Capt. Herriott (B Company), and Lieut. P. Cole (A Company) were, I think, in charge of the three companies.

men and transport. For a long time nothing happened, but eventually a German field battery fired several rapid salvoes of shells enfilading the road. Fortunately the greater number fell slightly wide of the road, but a few men in one of the Manchester battalions were hit. It was however a lucky escape. After this the road cleared quickly and we moved on into Fonquevillers. This village had been badly knocked about in the early days of the war, and few houses were in anything but ruins.

But there were still many cellars intact, and also a number of tin huts built for the French refugees in 1917. Officers of Battalion H.Q. were billeted in a cellar, and this was improved by mattresses, tables, and chairs brought in from the huts outside. Here in spite of intermittent shelling we got a much needed rest. But Fonquevillers was no place for a permanent rest cure. The village was shelled on and off all day, and several of our men were hit. I assisted the Adjutant, Capt. S.P. Brook-Booth, M.C., to collect a supply of early vegetables from the little gardens; and the officers in our reserve camp at Souastre thoughtfully sent up a couple of cooked chickens and a few other luxuries, so that evening we had something in the nature of a feast. Next morning, March 31, Lieut. Johnston, temporarily in command of A Company got a shell splinter through his hand and had to be sent back. I was then put in command of A Company and left Battalion H.Q., so that for some days the observers were not under my charge. About this time L.-C. Flynn, one of the observers, was seriously wounded by a shell, and we learnt later on that he died of his wounds. It was an unlucky affair, for he was one of the best observers. But I had no further casualties for a long time. I found A Company quartered in a line of old trenches between Gommecourt Wood and Fonquevillers. I believe they were part of the old British front line before the Somme battle started. Accommodation was very limited, and I found the other officers of A Company,[19] four in number, with their batmen and cook all crowded together in a small shelter. It was as may be imagined uncomfortably hot at times, especially during the night, part of which I spent in the trench outside. We only

19. Second-Lieuts. N. Holt, C.R. King, J. Dodds, and J. Lassey.

got a few shells from the enemy here, his attention was directed more to the village behind us and Gommecourt Wood in front.

On April 1 we got orders to proceed after dark to the front line trenches at Bucquoy - A Company was to hold those on the left, with B Company to their right. We were also given a route, but in the darkness it was difficult to find and it led to a curious incident on our journey forward. We assembled the company on the road outside Gommecourt and made towards the village as fast as the crowded state of the road would allow. Happily we were not shelled here, but there were signs on the road that others had not been so fortunate. When we reached Gommecourt, a mere ruin now of broken trees and buildings, we were clear of the press of transport and troops. We turned south-east hoping to strike a tramway running towards Biez Wood. Nothing, however, could we see of the tramway, and we could only push on, hoping to find it. After going on awhile we certainly seemed to be reaching a rather queer place, for we saw our men setting out wire, and a rather scared little man appeared out of the darkness and told us that 'Jerry was over there,' pointing down the road. We did not stop for this, but when a German Verey light shot up almost under our noses, we decided that we had indeed come too far and that it was time to turn back. This we did without waste of time and retraced our steps to Gommecourt. I was expecting any minute to hear a machine-gun open on us down the road. But if 'Jerry' was there in any force he had decided to keep quiet, and we got safely back to Gommecourt. After this experience we took a way that we knew, although it was not the one laid down for us. And after a long march in the dark we struck the Essarts-Bucquoy Road, and found our guides awaiting us on the road near Bucquoy. Whilst this relief was going on our field batteries kept up a hot fire on the enemy's front, but he made no reply.

The guides took us by a winding route through the north end of Bucquoy to the trenches, which consisted of an old German drain, very straight and about six feet deep. It ran parallel to the east side of the village and about 200 yards from its outskirts. The Company H.Q. lay a little way behind the front line and consisted of a short narrow slit in the ground, roofed over with tin - one of the smallest shelters I have ever been in. It was possible to sit down, but not to lie down, and the floor was inches deep in cold mud. Here I found two very disconsolate officers awaiting relief. They seemed to be nearly perished with the cold and wet, and quite worn out by their cheerless sojourn in the trenches. The trench lay on the slope of a slight hill, the crest being about 200 yards away. The enemy were not close, their position was out of sight and unknown. But to the left Logeast Wood was clearly visible, and the enemy were known to be there. Our trench ended abruptly on the left, and the nearest British troops on this flank were some way off and more to the east, so that there was a considerable gap in the line here. On the right of course we were in touch with B Company, who were commanded by Lieut. Affleck, M.C., a veteran of the Houthulst Forest battle, and one of our most redoubtable warriors in the 7th N.F. I knew that I need not worry about my right flank! No smoke from fires could be allowed in the trenches, and cooking had to be done over small fires of fine wood splinters. When morning came it was possible to have a better look round. All the reserve ammunition, about 5000 rounds, had been pulled out of the boxes, and the bandoliers were mostly buried in the mud. It was a great business clearing the trench of mud and salvaging and cleaning the ammunition. The enemy did not know where we were. All morning three of his aeroplanes, flying low, hovered about our little trench, occasionally firing bursts at us with their machine-guns. We only replied with an occasional shot, and of course they could not tell where that came from. At any rate the German guns let the trench alone and poured a stream of heavy shells all day and night into the village behind us and into the hedges at the east end. The fact appeared quite clearly later on that the enemy could not locate our front line. A messenger dog, belonging to the enemy, was captured at this time near Bucquoy, bearing a message in German as follows: 'The affair of Bucquoy is off for the present, as we don't know where Tommy is.' It was well indeed for our two companies that the drain trench was not suspected by the enemy. There were no traverses in it from one end to the other, and a very few well-aimed shells would have blown us to pieces.

That night (April 2) the British forces made a counter-attack at Ayette and drove the enemy as far back as the old hangars at Moyenneville. Seen from the trenches at Bucquoy it was a fine sight. The enemy put up all kinds of coloured lights, including silhouette lights and 'flaming onions' both orange and mauve.

Meanwhile we of the 7th N.F. undertook a small venture against certain parties of the enemy that had been seen and sniped at from B Company's trench. These parties were busy digging trenches about 400 yards away to our front. Soon after dark 2nd-Lieuts. J. Dodds and J.H. Edmunds took out a raiding party of over twenty men in order to secure a prisoner if possible. As it turned out this was done quickly enough and without firing a shot.

For on the party creeping forward to the wire belt at the top of the hill, a German N.C.O. walked towards them, was surprised by 2nd-Lieut. Dodds, and surrendered without a struggle. He was already slightly wounded, and had come forward perhaps to have a look at the wire. He was brought back at once to the trench, and it fell to me to examine the man and to remove all papers from him except his pay-book and identity disc. I went out and examined him in a mixture of such broken French and German as I could summon at so short a notice. I also went through his papers with the aid of lighted matches. After this he was sent down under escort to Battalion H.Q., and thence to D.H.Q.

It proved to be a useful capture, for it showed that a fresh German division had arrived opposite our front. Later on 2nd-Lieut. Dodds was awarded the Military Cross for the capture. Early next morning (April 3) the Division sent orders that I should return with the Divisional observers to the rear. So I left the trench in charge of 2nd-Lieut. N. Holt and went back with my servant through Bucquoy, taking care to avoid certain large shells which were falling every now and then about the village. Calling at Battalion H.Q. I found that the observers were now in some trenches about half a mile farther back in the direction of Essarts. I soon found them, however, and whilst waiting for them to get ready I was hospitably supplied with some whisky and soda by the officers of one of the Lancashire Regiments.

At last we set off in small parties towards Gommecourt, our destination being Souastre, a long march for tired men. Whilst passing Biez Wood we came in for some rather unpleasant attention from the enemy's artillery, whose observers could see movement at this spot all too well. However we got away at last without mishap and collected again short of Gommecourt, where we halted for a meal of bully and biscuit. Eventually after passing through Gommecourt and Fonquevillers we struggled on to Souastre, very footsore and completely worn out.

From March 23 onwards it had been one long strain, heavy marching most days and, with few exceptions, sleepless nights. For myself I was a very tramp, boots worn to pieces, clothes hanging with mud, and thick with mud up to the eyes. Undoubtedly it was the most trying experience physically that I have ever been through. At Souastre I called at rear Battalion H.Q., where Capt. Herriott of B Company kindly lent me his rubber boots and some clean socks, a great luxury and comfort. Then I went on to the Officers' Hut at the battalion reserve camp, and was able to lie down and sleep till well on into the next day. Souastre was not a bad place to rest, for it was shelled only very occasionally with long-range guns.

The following afternoon (April 4) Capt. Kirsopp came to see me and he brought a motor-car. He wished to reconnoitre a 'battle O.P.,' i.e. a place in the back area from which to observe enemy shelling of the forward areas or enemy attacks on our line. I was told that things were expected to happen next day; and I was instructed to find a post where I could see what was going on, somewhere in the neighbourhood of the Château de la Haie.

In the morning (April 5) I went with Corp. Walker and L.-C. Cowen to the Bayencourt Ridge, south of the château, and we got into a small trench. Things certainly were happening, for the enemy was scattering his heavy high-velocity shells broadcast over the country. He seemed to direct them chiefly against our battery positions and the roads and trenches in rear of Fonquevillers and Sailly-au-Bois. The number of these shells was unusually large; but later on towards 10 A.M. things began to quieten down in the back area. What had happened was this.

The 37th Division with the assistance of tanks made a counter-attack on Rossignol Wood. The Germans had prepared to make another of their grand attacks that same morning. But it was anticipated by about half an hour. The result was a fierce struggle in which we gained a little ground and a certain number of prisoners. The German attack therefore came to nothing, and this proved to be his last attempt of a serious kind on our part of the front. Anxiety was not however, at an end for many days to come.

During the next few days the observers held a battle O.P. near the orchard in Fonquevillers. It was a long walk from Souastre and back, but fairly quiet, for it could be reached by going across country and avoiding the sorely harassed roads.

On April 8 the 42nd Division was taken back for a short rest to the area round Authie.

CHAPTER XXXII

TRENCH WARFARE - HÉBUTERNE

DURING DIVISIONAL REST the observers were attached for rations and accommodation to the H.Q. Company of the 7th N.F. We marched back, therefore, with the battalion through Couin and St. Leger to Authie. We found nice billets awaiting us in this pleasant French village, which was too far from the enemy to be afflicted with shell fire. It was full of French civilians, and the small shops had various little luxuries to which we had been unused for some time. From Authie Woods to Bayencourt ran the 'Red Line' trenches, a sort of 'last-but-one' reserve line, which had been hastily dug by Chinese labourers and were still only about four feet deep. We did not stay long at Authie, for the billets were wanted to accommodate French troops who were being hurried northwards to the battle now raging about Kemmel.

On April 12 the 7th N.F. moved forward to the village of Coigneux and H.Q. were established in a French estaminet. There were civilians here too, but the village was liable to be shelled and half of them had gone away. A distressing attack of tooth-ache took me twice to the C.C.S. near Doullens. I found that town more deserted than it used to be, for the Germans had shelled and bombed it vigorously since their offensive started.

On April 16, after a week's rest, the 42nd Division took over the trenches running from Gommecourt to Hébuterne. The same day the observers moved to some old trenches north of the Château de la Haie. It was a cold place in wet weather, and we were occasionally shelled. But after a few days through the kindness of Col. Guy, the G.S.O. I, billets were found for us in a cottage at Bayencourt, which lies about half a mile south of the château. It was indeed a pleasant oasis in a badly shelled area. Why the enemy left the place alone I cannot say. But when we got there there were still plenty of old French folk, who lived quietly on amid the surrounding strife, and continued to keep their cows in the fields and to cultivate the land. The church had not been shelled, for a wonder, and the clock was still going and striking the hours.

The observers sent up two parties of two men every day to an O.P. north-east of Hébuterne. The other men manned a battle O.P. on the Bayencourt Ridge during the morning.

April 23, St. George's Day, provided a little excitement for three of us. We were told to try to find an O.P. near the Quarries at Hébuterne, not generally a very healthy spot. As we were shelled incessantly all the time we were near the place, the idea of establishing a post here was abandoned. And eventually another post was fixed on, on the north-east side of Hébuterne. Some useful work was done here by the observers; they obtained some valuable information about enemy movement and got the artillery to shell a relief that was taking place. At the close of our tour in the line, which occurred about May 4, the IV Corps directed all Infantry observers to take sound bearings of enemy guns and to wire them at once to the Counter-Battery Office. This was gratifying, as we had made a special effort to report these sound bearings, a system of which I had learnt something in the Salient.

From May 4 to June 9 the Division remained in the rest area about Couin. The observers left Bayencourt and joined the 7th N.F. at Coigneux, where we lived in tents on the high chalky ground south of Rossignol Farm. I messed with the officers of A Company, and shared a tent with Lieut W.H. Fisher and 2nd-Lieut Dodd. Owing to the bombing and shelling in the neighbourhood, we were ordered to fortify our tents. So we had a small trench dug for each inside the tent and in these we put our valises. It was rather like a shallow grave, but it gave you a feeling of security when bits were flying about. During this month the observers had a little mild training each day; but the G.O.C. sent word to me to rest the men as much as possible. I amused myself at the battle O.P. on

Bayencourt Ridge and sent in daily reports of sound bearings to the IV Corps Counter-Battery Office.

On the whole the enemy let our camp fairly well alone. We had one large bomb dropped in the camp, but it failed to do any material damage. Latterly the 4-inch naval guns took to sending a few shells over daily, but we had only a few men wounded from splinters. Other units near us came off worse. During the rest at Coigneux we had a visit from some American troops. I think they had come to gain a little mild experience of our methods. Anyway a small party of their observers came to see how we held our posts. And they were taken to the battle O.P. and to the forward O.P. at Hébuterne.

CHAPTER XXXIII

TRENCH WARFARE - THE COLINCAMPS RIDGE

NO OFFENSIVE OPERATIONS on a large scale were undertaken against the enemy on the IV Corps front, Bucquoy to Auchonvillers, before the middle of August 1918. The period from May onwards was spent in strengthening the defences and in wearing down the enemy's strength and morale. The latter object was achieved by continual harassing fire from our guns, strong counter-battery, periodical gas projections, bombing from our aeroplanes, and raids. It was still necessary to work hard on our defences, for the German offensive was by no means over, and it was impossible to say at what moment the enemy might renew his attacks on this part of the front.

The part played by the Divisional observers during this period of trench warfare was more important and useful than at any other period of their employment. This was partly due to the excellent position for ground observation on the ridge between Colincamps and Auchonvillers, and partly to the improvement in means of communication with D.H.Q. and the artillery. Great credit is due to Capt. Kirsopp for his continual efforts to make the information obtained more rapid and effective. And also to the men who got the information by patiently sticking to their job for ten long weeks, sometimes under trying and discouraging conditions.

The observers were quartered in a number of small shelters on the high ground between Coigneux and Bus, well back from the shelled and bombed area. The shelters were in the side of a green mound, near

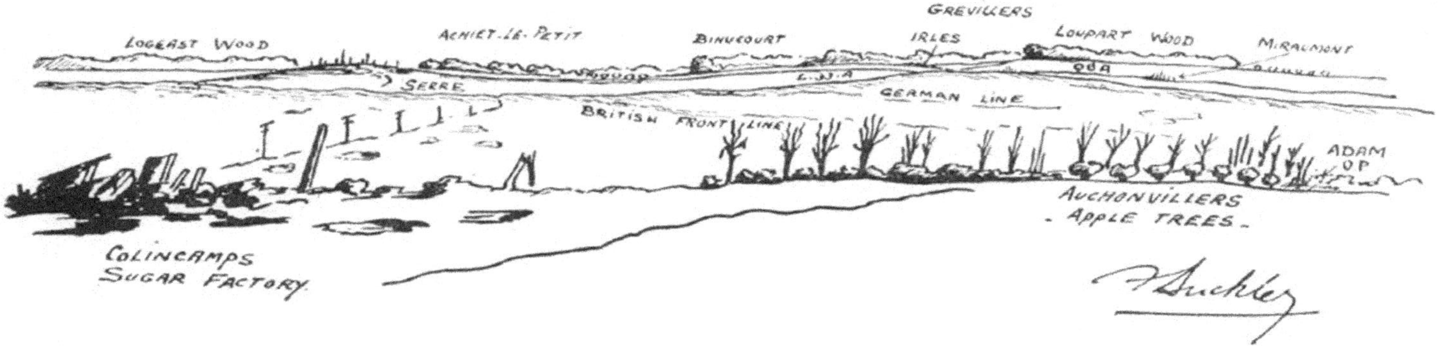

Panorama from Adam O.P., July 1918.

the Bus waterworks; and this place was used as a battle O.P. and became known as 'Eve' O.P. From here there was a splendid view of the country just behind the British front line. So that the observers stationed here could say at once where heavy shelling was going on, either by day or by night. A telephone connected 'Eve' O.P. with D.H.Q. and also with the forward O.P. The latter post was about four miles away in a small trench on the ridge north of Auchonvillers near some apple trees, which perhaps suggested the name 'Adam' O.P. In many ways it was an admirable place for an O.P. If care was taken it could be approached without being seen by the enemy. It was screened by a thick hedge and also by a deep belt of wire about thirty yards in front of the hedge. The O.P. itself was in the hedge bank, and was roofed over with several small 'elephant' shelters, with earth on top of them. There was plenty of room for at least three men to work inside. And observation was obtained through a small opening in the hedge bank. The opening was always further screened by sandbags, so that only the end of the telescope was exposed to the enemy and that was always in a deep shadow. A few yards away outside the O.P. in the trench was a small mined dugout. This was not very deep, about six feet down at the most; but it was under the roots of the hedge, a good protection against the shells of field guns. In this dugout the observers who were not on duty were able to sleep, and the men in the O.P. could take refuge in case of heavy shelling. The O.P. was connected by telephone with D.H.Q. and also with Eve O.P. Not far away in the same trench there were other O.P.'s, one held by the Lovat Scouts (Corps Observers) and another, 'Rose' O.P., by the heavy artillery.

Our method of working the two O.P.'s was as follows. The N.C.O., L.-C. Cowen, remained at Eve O.P. and assisted me with various duties there, and with the duty of inspecting the working of Adam O.P. The other observers, eight in number, were divided into two groups of four, one in charge of Pte. J. King and the other one in charge of Pte. W.O.S. Fail. Three observers from No. 1 group went forward to Adam O.P. and stayed there for forty-eight hours, drawing their rations each day from the nearest Battalion H.Q. After this they were relieved by three observers from No 2 group and so on. By this arrangement I was able to rest the men and to carry on observation continuously for ten weeks without unduly tiring the men. Out of the four observers in a group, only three were at Adam O.P. at the same time, the fourth man remaining back at Eve O.P. for a rest. Thus during sixteen days each observer had three tours of duty at Adam O.P. lasting two days each, two rests of two days, and then a rest of six days. This kept all the men fresh, an important matter if you wish for good observation.

At Adam O.P. two of the three observers were always at the telescope during daylight, and one was resting in the dugout. And at night one had to remain awake, to be able to report heavy shelling to D.H.Q. and to act as gas sentry for the others. It was of course all done in a system of reliefs amongst themselves. During these summer months observation was possible in the most favourable circumstances from 3.45 A.M. to 9.10 P.M., so the night was comparatively short. Adam O.P. was visited on alternate days by L.-C. Cowen and myself. I went invariably in the early morning, so as to arrive at the O.P. about an hour or so after observation had become possible. The enemy exposed himself more freely during the two or three hours after dawn than at any other time during the day. By going up early I was able to see that the men were at their post at this important time, and to get their early information, often of importance, as soon as possible. It meant starting in the dark, and often a cold wet journey across country, but the good fellows at the O.P. always had a cup of tea for me - a little act of kindness which illustrates our friendly relations.

The most interesting things we could see from Adam O.P. were the German front line trenches south and south-west of Serre, two spots known as 'L. 33. a. O. 9.' and 'Q. 6. a. 9. 8.' where anyone approaching these forward trenches had to cross a ridge and so come under our observation, the German transport roads about Achiet-le-Petit, Irles, and Loupart Wood. The German front line was within 2000 yards, Q. 6. a. within 4000 yards, L. 33. a. rather over 6000 yards, and the roads well over 10,000 yards away. Near to Pys was a German C.C.S., which was narrowly watched, for any increase in its size would have probably meant preparation for an attack. And behind Irles was a derelict British tank which the Germans used as an O.P., for it was invariably visited by a number of men just before one of their reliefs took place, and at no other time.

Every day two reports were sent in to D.H.Q. of all movement seen during the preceding twelve hours. And every movement seen was entered into a Log Book. This was my special department; and after a time it was possible to compile a further book called the Summary Book, with coloured charts of daily movement. In a short time we discovered the average or normal movement for the twenty-four hours. And after that it was quite simple to warn the Division at once whenever any movement of an abnormal character was taking place.

Owing to weak eyesight I could not do much telescope work myself - my part of the field work was map reading, in which I had considerable assistance from aeroplane photographs at D.H.Q. I asked the observers to make telescopic sketches, on every compass bearing, of what they could see. And then from these sketches and with my own maps and protractor I was able to tell them what they were looking at on the map, and to prepare a panoramic sketch for their use at Adam O.P. Pte. King sent in an admirable series of sketches which were most useful in this work of discovery. Later on the more powerful telescope was also taken up to Adam O.P., and with this Pte. Fail did some most useful work. With his exceptional eyesight and a gift for sketching he made a series of excellent artillery target sketches. These I copied out and coloured and sent to D.H.Q.; and they were sent on to the IV Corps Heavy Artillery. These targets were fired at with great success. For example one of the first sent in was of a cook-house and wireless station at L. 33. a. On July 11 the heavy artillery carried out a successful shoot on the place, using Adam O.P. as their observing station. In order to place on record some of the work done by my observers at Adam O.P. I will give some of the results of their systematic observation.

A Divisional relief on July 3 and 4 was spotted by Capt. Kirsopp on information given by the observers of exceptional movement in the forward area. Another Divisional relief was detected by largely increased movement on July 25. And a battalion relief on August 6, with disastrous results for the enemy. At least fifty copies of different telescopic sketches were sent in to the Division, including a series of eight showing new workings by the Germans in their front line system. Reports of nearly seventy gun-flashes were sent in as well as many sound bearing reports. The following numbers of German infantry and transport vehicles were reported from Adam O.P.

Month	Days	Days of Bad Light	Effective Days	Infantry Seen	Transport Vehicles
June	21	8	13	2,100	83
July	31	7	24	5,400	413
August	20	4	16	4,650	205
Total	**72**	**19**	**53**	**12,150**	**791**

Our two best days occurred on August 6 and 12. On the 6th a large movement was observed in the early hours, indicating a relief, which was reported to the Division at once by wire. So that when the relief was continued at night, our artillery were prepared to deal with the German parties moving in or out of the trenches. On this day alone 1126 infantry and 55 transport vehicles were seen on the move. The 42nd Division Intelligence Report of August 7 reported the matter as follows:

> 'Relief south of the Serre-Mailly Road which commenced on a large scale on the morning of the 6th was continued during the evening; between 6.50 and 8.20 P.M. 197 men with packs in nineteen parties came towards the front line past Q. 6. a. 95. 80. These parties were engaged by H.A. with great success. Casualties caused being estimated to be at least fifty; four direct hits were obtained on a party at 7.15 P.M., and on one occasion an out-going party was seen to have a free fight with an in-going party to gain possession of a sunken track or trench in Q. 6. a. Total hostile infantry seen by Divisional O.P. on the 6th reached the high number of 1126.'

The observers had their share in those fifty casualties, as Pte. F. Turner went to Rose O.P. and directed the Sergeant Gunner in charge to the proper map reference of the German troops. That 6-inch battery shot superbly, and I wish I knew the Sergeant's name. The G.O.C. sent his congratulations to the observers on the day's work.

On August 12 at 6 A.M. the observers informed me that the Germans had been seen going out of their trenches in large numbers and all carrying packs, rifles, and boxes as well. On this I sent a pigeon message to the Corps, saying that the enemy might be retiring now. As it happened this was quite correct, as the Germans admitted themselves a few days later in their communiqué.

I also wish to put on record an act of kindness to the observers by the Division and Corps. On August 8 the enemy began to shell the neighbourhood of Adam O.P. rather severely with a 5.9-inch howitzer battery. As this went on, I rang up D.H.Q. and asked if anything could be done in retaliation against the enemy's O.P.'s in L. 33. a. Col. Guy told me that he would see what the Corps would do for us; and rang up later to tell me to ask the observers at Adam O.P. to note results at 2.30 P.M. At the appointed time, every active heavy gun in the Corps fired a shell simultaneously against selected targets, including L. 33. a. There were at least four brigades of heavies in the Corps and the noise was colossal. It must have astonished the enemy as much as it did me.

On August 9, 2nd-Lieut. Edmunds of the 7th N.F. came to assist me, and to take over command of the observers during my leave which was now drawing near. I told him that we had never been shelled at Eve O.P. But as luck would have it that very afternoon, about 2 P.M., a long-range gun shelled the O.P. for about twenty minutes; and I had to clear the men off into the neighbouring Red Line trenches till the annoyance ceased.

On August 14 the enemy were attacked all along the IV Corps front and a considerable advance was made that day. Pte. King remained at the telescope all day, and sent in a number of interesting reports about the enemy's movements.

At this point I have to break off the narrative, as my leave warrant arrived that night and I left the observers till August 31 in charge of 2nd-Lieut. J.H. Edmunds.

One word about the admirable services of my batman, Pte. W. Critchlow. For ten weeks and more, in addition to looking after my own personal comforts, he cooked for the whole party of observers at Eve O.P. This may seem a small matter, but he never had a rest like the other men, and his hard work contributed materially to the comfort and efficiency of the section.

CHAPTER XXXIV

THE BRITISH OFFENSIVE 1918 - BAPAUME RETAKEN

On **MY RETURN** to France, I reached Authieule railway station on August 31, and went on next morning, partly by car and motor-bus and partly on foot, to Miraumont. Here I found the observers with B Company (Capt. W.N. Craigs, M.C.) of the 7th N.F. near the railway station. It had been strange passing over the smitten ground on the Serre Ridge, and it was possible then to realise the terrible effects of our heavy shell fire. Gangs of men were now mending the road all the way to Miraumont; but it must have been in a shocking state. In one place part of a transport cart hung suspended from the shattered branches of a tree; and everywhere the ground was absolutely churned to pieces.

I learnt that D.H.Q. had moved forward to Grevillers, and on September 3 I decided to make a move forward to Loupart Wood, in order to get the observers more in touch with them.

We were badly handicapped in all the succeeding stages of the campaign by having no transport to move our belongings. Besides the ordinary infantryman's equipment, no light weight, we had our blankets, three telescopes, compasses, and a lot of maps, books, and stationery, and our daily ration to carry as well. By good luck, however, we found an old German hand-cart in very fair condition about the station yard; and we used this hand-cart for getting our gear along for many a weary mile. In fact we finally dropped it at Le Quesnoy on November 5, not because it was worn out, but because other transport was found for us.

By the evening of September 3 we got settled into some dugouts at the north end of Loupart Wood. There were a few dead Germans scattered about, but a lot more dead horses than men. And as the weather was hot, the air was none too pleasant.

Next day I visited D.H.Q. who were in some tents outside Grevillers, and Capt. Kirsopp told me that the observers were urgently needed. It was proposed to send a party of them forward on bicycles to keep in touch with the retreating Germans. And so the same day Ptes. King and Drake (7th N.F.) and F. Greenwood (10th M.B.) went forward towards Havrincourt Wood to get such news as they could. It had been intended at first that I should go with them, but it was found impossible to provide me with a horse. The British forces had already taken Bapaume, Villers-au-Flos, and Riencourt, and the enemy were supposed to be retreating fast in the direction of the old Hindenburg Line which lay beyond Havrincourt Wood. Pte. King's party did good work; they went through Barastre and Bus in front of the advance guards of the infantry, and met with no opposition beyond occasional long-range machine-gun fire. Their first O.P. was just south of Bertincourt, and the following days near Neuville-Bourjonval. For this expedition Pte. King was awarded the Military Medal. On September 3 I went with Pte. Turner to some high ground just south of Bapaume and stayed there several hours. From here little shelling could be seen, the main body of the enemy must have retired as far as Havrincourt Wood. Long-range shells fell near Bapaume and the railway during the day. The same evening I reported at D.H.Q., and found things pretty lively during my visit; for two or three German 'planes dropped a number of bombs about the place, not a pleasant experience for those living in tents. Next day (September 4) the observers moved forward with the hand-cart through Grevillers and then to Thilloy and across country to the high ground south of Bapaume. Here there were plenty of small German shelters and dugouts partially protected by a shallow trench. In these we took up our quarters, whilst D.H.Q. moved to some ammunition dugouts on the other side of the road from Bapaume to Peronne. Next day (September 5) accompanied by Pte. Turner I reconnoitred the high ground about Bus. There were many German dead still lying about near the approaches to Villers-au-Flos, where a considerable stand must have been made by the German machine-gunners to cover the retreat. Also we saw on our way back a party of the 7th N.F. preparing to bury a number of our own men who had fallen in the advance. The same evening I was told that the 42nd Division would be relieved that night by the New Zealand Division, and that the observers should stand fast until further orders, Pte. King's party joined us the next day. We stayed here for the next two weeks, in what proved to be quite comfortable quarters. A German soda-water factory was discovered at Beaulencourt, and we were in time to secure a few bottles. Training was now resumed in the mornings, and the observers practised sending and receiving messages with four signallers of the 7th N.F. who were attached to us. In the afternoon we were free to roam over the recent battle-field, where many souvenirs of the enemy could be picked up. We now lay just to the north of the old Somme battle-ground. And on September 15 I went to Martinpuich by bus down the Albert-Bapaume Road and revisited the scene of our attack on the High Wood Ridge, which had taken place just two years before. During our stay at this place we had visits every night from German aircraft. But they fared none too well. I saw one aeroplane brought down in flames at night near Villers-au-Flos by our anti-aircraft guns; and two others shared the same fate. This was a great feather in the cap of the anti-aircraft gunners; for an aeroplane is particularly difficult to hit at night.

The 42nd Division was ordered to relieve the 37th Division on September 22. The latter Division had now reached the old British front line east of Havrincourt Wood. And the Germans were now in the Hindenburg Line, behind 'the walls of bronze' which had checked us once and which they hoped would again stay the pursuit of their beaten legions.

One particularly disgusting feature of our journey in pursuit of the enemy was the dreadful state of the huts he had occupied. They all appeared to be moving with lice and fleas, and it was a most difficult matter to keep oneself free from their unpleasant attentions. It was the same wherever we stopped.

CHAPTER XXXV

THE STORMING OF THE HINDENBURG LINE NEAR TRESCAULT

ON SEPTEMBER 20 I went with Lieut. G.F. Doble, the Divisional Intelligence Officer, to visit the new area in front. We found D.H.Q. established in a wonderful series of huts south-west of Vélu Wood. These had been the H.Q. of some German Corps, and wonderfully well barricaded they were. Inside each hut, which was panelled with wood, there was a sliding panel which admitted to a deep shelter dugout beneath. Here in case of bombing by our aeroplanes, the German officer had been able to retire quickly and without loss of dignity to a place of safety. From here we paid a short visit by motor-car to the B.H.Q. north-west of Havrincourt Wood. On returning through Bapaume I had the great pleasure of meeting Major W. Anderson, D.S.O., M.C., my old Brigade-Major, who was now G.S.O. II of the 37th Division.

On September 21 the observers went forward with their hand-cart through Riencourt, Villers-au-Flos, and Haplincourt to the outskirts of Bertincourt. We first selected some empty huts near Vélu Wood as our place of residence. But as we were shelled about five minutes after arriving, we decided to move a little farther from the wood. Finally we found two useful Nissen huts built into the roadside and sheltered by some tall elm trees, just west of Bertincourt. It was not a very quiet or healthy spot anywhere near Bertincourt; but we were not damaged by the enemy's shells, though occasionally annoyed. The same afternoon I went forward by myself to reconnoitre a position for the Divisional O.P.

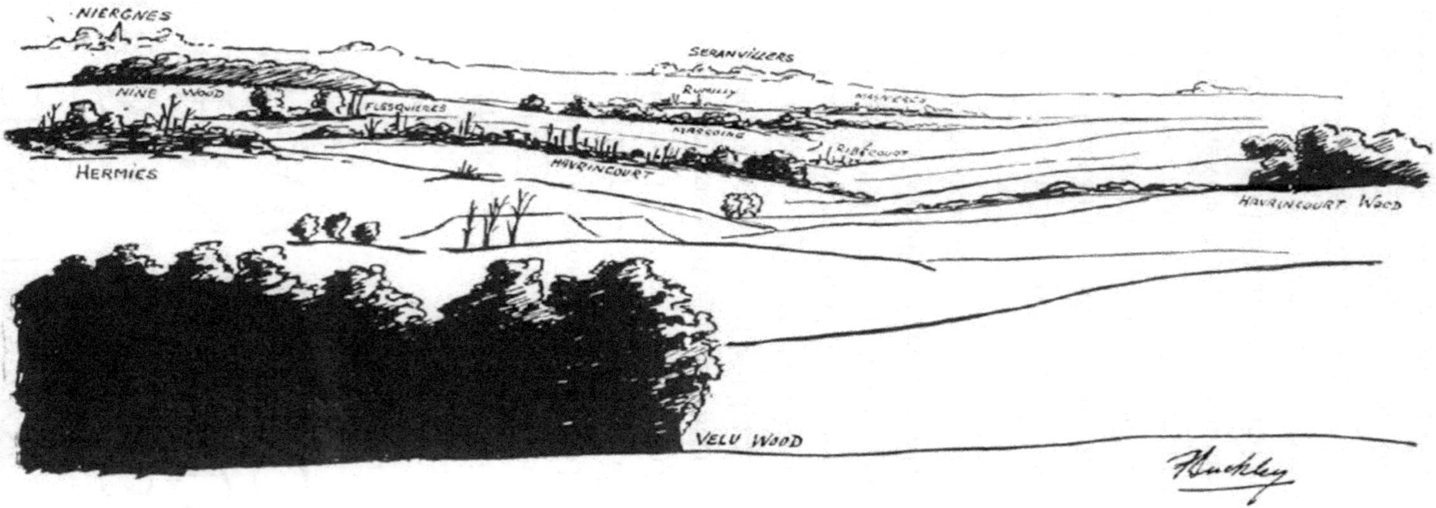

Scene of the Attack on the Hindenburg Line, Sept. 28, 1918.

And I found a useful place in the north of Havrincourt Wood, or rather in the rough thorny scrub that had once formed part of the wood.

Observation was obtained through the branches of a tree, and a small shelter dugout was close at hand. The field of view extended along the left flank of the Corps and Divisional front, and went a long way back to the high ground between Niergnes and Esnes. Flesquières, Ribécourt, Marcoing, Rumilly, and Masnières could all be seen. The next few days were spent in locating our surroundings and in reporting the traffic seen on the back roads. On September 27 I went with L.-C. Cowen to inspect an O.P. in the British front-line system south-east of Trescault. We went through the wood and then along a winding C.T. which brought us to the front line. Here we found a deep dugout with a ladder leading up to an O.P. on ground level. The view in front was not altogether satisfactory, but towards the left it was good.

At dawn on September 28 the grand assault on the Hindenburg Line began. It was quite successful on our left and on the left of our front, but the Division on our right had great difficulty in getting forward. By the following day, however, the line was advanced along the whole front, and the N.Z. Division, taking over the pursuit from us, made good captures of men and guns. L.-C. Cowen and Pte. McGarrigle went to the O.P. in the front line on September 28 and had rather a rough passage. Pte. Fail had a small party at the other O.P., and obtained a fairly good view of the battle. On September 29 Pte. King went with Pte. Chappell in the direction of Ribécourt, but this expedition was brought to an end by a shell which wounded Pte. Chappell badly in the face. This was the second and, as events turned out, the last casualty amongst my observers. I spent a long time the second day with the observers at the O.P. in Havrincourt Wood and we saw much German transport hurrying back south of Niergnes. On the night of September 29 the 42nd Division was relieved, and I received instructions to remain at our quarters near Bertincourt. After the battle we were no longer troubled with any shells. Second-Lieut. Edmunds who had been on leave since we left Miraumont came back to assist me, for about another month. Great droves of German prisoners now began to pass us several times a day, a cheering sight in one way, but not a pleasant one in another. They were truly a desperate-looking collection of men, mostly of a very low class.

This halt enabled me to get round the country and make sketches of the various battle-fields.

One night I had dinner at D.H.Q. as the guest of Capt. Kirsopp, and enjoyed the hospitality of 'Z' Mess. I found a great curiosity in the fields near Bertincourt. An old cannon-ball pitted with rust and dating possibly from Marlborough's days. As I could not take it away with me, I gave it to Major Clarke, the G.S.O. II.

On October 7 the observers moved to some dugouts near Trescault, where we remained two days. On October 8 I went on to Welsh Ridge, but nothing much could be seen from there. The battle-field was strewn with Germans who had fallen in the battle ten days before. On October 9 we had a long march which took all day. We went through Beaucamp and then towards Masnières, finally reaching the shattered village of Crèvecœur. Next morning we moved on again to Esnes, where we had billets in a nice farm-house.

At last we had reached the land of vegetables, and for the rest of the campaign we had a plentiful supply. We had been very short of this kind of food since May.

On October 11 we moved on again and got a billet in a small cottage in Fontaine-au-Pire. Next day on again to the next town, Beauvois, which was not at all badly smashed. We had billets in a couple of small cottages off the main street and we were fairly comfortable here. The plague of house-flies was very bad at this place; the whole place was full of them.

The 42nd Division relieved the N.Z. Division on October 12 on a front extending south of Solesmes and covering Briastre.

CHAPTER XXXVI

THE GERMANS' LAST STAND

ON OCTOBER 12 I went with Pte. Firth to a ridge south of Viesly to look for an O.P., and selected a spot in the open, but near a sunk road. However, the G.O.C. required a post to be held on the high ground north of the village. This was only half a mile from the enemy's front line and in full view of the enemy, so that I suspected we should not be allowed to stop there very long. A regiment of Hussars was attached to the Corps and stationed at Caudry.

It was arranged that an officer and six observers from this regiment should work in conjunction with the Divisional observers. These mounted men were particularly useful in getting messages back quickly from the O.P. to a report centre, for during this open warfare it was impossible to connect the observers by telephone to D.H.Q.

The first day at the O.P. north of Viesly passed quietly enough, and Ptes. King and McGarrigle made a useful sketch of the view in front. Next day, when I went up to the O.P. to make additions to the sketch, conditions were not very good. Our only cover was a shallow trench about one foot deep; and for an hour whilst I was trying to sketch the details of the landscape the enemy's 4.2-inch howitzers shelled the hill persistently. I told the observers, when I went back, to leave this post if things got no better and to man the post south of Viesly. And this was done soon afterwards, as the shells began to fall very close. Unfortunately from now onwards the light was no good for long-range observation. Day after day the country was covered with a thick white mist, a common experience in October, which made observation quite out of the question. However, from the sketches that had been made, I was able to make a drawing of the panorama in front, which was printed out for the use of the troops in the line.

It was decided to attack the German positions at midnight on October 19-20. Taking advantage of the heavy mist the British field artillery placed their guns in two long lines, twenty-eight guns in a line and almost wheel to wheel, behind the ridges south of Viesly. This was an extraordinary sight, for they had no cover whatever except the thick white mist overhead. Behind the second row, there was a battery of heavy howitzers (8- or 9-inch calibre), and a little farther back several batteries of 60-pounder guns. The night attack was carried out by the 126th Infantry Brigade and was wonderfully successful.

At 10 A.M. on October 20 I called at B.H.Q., a house in Prayelle, to get the latest news. Then I joined Ptes. Fail and Greenwood at the O.P., which was now under the muzzles of the field guns. We left this post and went towards Briastre, and, crossing the road from Viesly, we finally selected a position near the Briastre Cemetery. Just across the valley the enemy's guns were pounding the positions we had won that morning. It was in preparation for a counter-attack, which, however, was crushed by the fire from our own artillery. We sent in several situation reports to D.H.Q. through the H.Q. of the 10th Manchester Regiment, which were now in a cutting not far from the cemetery.

On my way back to Beauvois I met a number of tanks travelling slowly forward towards Viesly; but I believe they were unable to get across the River Selle that night. For the next two days the observers held a post on the north side of Viesly; and on October 23 the 42nd Division attacked again, the N.Z. Division taking up the pursuit of the enemy about midday. The men of the 42nd Division have every reason to be proud of their battle at Solesmes; the Germans were very strongly entrenched and they were picked troops, and a night attack is, of course, one of the most difficult of all to carry out successfully.

The observers were instructed to remain at their quarters in Beauvois, and for the next eleven days training was resumed. I was told that great advantages might be obtained from panoramic sketches, if rapidly and accurately drawn by the observers. And so I directed most of the training here towards making these sketches. There was nothing in training that the men liked better than that.

During our rest at Beauvois the New Zealanders had pushed the Germans farther back, to the outskirts of Le Quesnoy, and towards the end of October we were warned that the 42nd Division would relieve them after a further attack.

CHAPTER XXXVII

THE FINAL RUSH FORWARD

ON NOVEMBER 3 I moved with the observers to the village of Viesly and got a billet in a cottage. The village had been badly mauled by the German guns during the recent fighting. The German does not behave nicely when his nerves are shaken, and we heard stories of ill-treatment of women in Solesmes.

Next day we went towards Romeries to reconnoitre the roads, and on November 5 we had a long march in the rain. Hitherto we had been lucky to have fine weather for trekking, but now it began to rain almost every day. We went on over crowded roads through Briastre, Solesmes, Romeries, and Beaudignies. At the latter place our heavy guns were still firing, for the Germans had only been pushed out of Le Quesnoy that morning, and their main body was retreating through the Mormal Forest. Our advance party, L.-C. Cowen and Pte. Addinall, who had gone forward on bicycles to find a billet in Le Quesnoy, met with a very warm reception from the French civilians in the town. After a little trouble I managed to get possession of a nice empty house near the railway station, where we were glad to turn in and get our clothes dry. Next day I went to D.H.Q. at Potelle, a moated farm or château.

There was some idea of disbanding the observers at this time, for Capt. Kirsopp found difficulty in getting us forward fast enough to be of any use. However the G.O.C. would not hear of it, and said the D.A.Q.M.G. must arrange to transport our things.

The same day I went forward to the advanced B.H.Q. at Forester's Point, on the N.W. side of the forest, east of Carnoy. And I arranged with the Brigade-Major of the 126th Infantry Brigade to send some of the observers to help him next day. This, however, was cancelled, as the Germans began to retreat towards the River Sambre. I saw some French children still about the cottages near the Mormal Forest, though there was still shelling going on. Coming back I avoided the village of Carnoy, as it was being heavily shelled by the enemy's long-range guns. This was the last time I came anywhere near the enemy's shell fire. The German dead lay in little clusters in the fields east of Le Quesnoy, and at various points along the railway.

On November 7 I moved my quarters to a small house at Herbignies, our belongings being brought for us by Divisional transport. Our hand-cart was finally dumped at Le Quesnoy. The next day I sent a small party of observers through the forest to Petit Bavay, and also detached Ptes. Fail, Ewart, and Austin for duty on the following day, sending them with bicycles to the Q.M. of the 7th N.F. at Petit Bavay. Also I walked through the forest to D.H.Q. at the same place. It was a long tramp in the mud, and I was thoroughly tired out when I reached Herbignies again that night.

On November 9 we had our final trek forward, some fifteen miles through the most glutinous mud. As the observers had been overlooked when the Divisional transport left Potelle, we had now to transport all our belongings as best we could without the aid of the hand-cart. This unfortunately meant dumping all our stores except such as were absolutely essential; and I lost a number of interesting records, maps, &c., in this way.

We loaded ourselves up then with everything we could take - very full packs and a blanket rolled on top, about the heaviest marching-order possible. By midday we had got through the forest to Petit Bavay, where we halted for a meal on the road side. Then we went on through Vieux Mesnil, where we had to ford the river, as the bridge was destroyed. On through Neuf Mesnil and at last to Hautmont. I was glad to get a billet in the first empty house I came to, 135 Rue de Gambetta. No beds, but a moderately clean floor to sleep on. Pte. Fail's party rejoined me here. They had gone right on to the firing line on the north bank of the River

Sambre, where the Guards were advancing. They brought back useful information as to what had been going on.

After disputing the crossing of the Sambre the Germans fled rapidly for about eight miles, and gave no further trouble beyond shelling the villages of Quievelon and Ferrière. Cyclists and cavalry were pushed out to keep in touch with them, but owing to the difficulties of transport the infantry could get no farther. There was now a general feeling that the end was not far off.

On November 10 I was told at D.H.Q. that there was a 'holiday air' about every one, and that nothing further need be done by the observers. Early next morning I heard two transport drivers discussing the situation in the road outside. They were quite convinced that the war was over. And they were right; a little later I got the message from D.H.Q. 'hostilities will cease at 11 A.M. to-day.' Heavy firing was still going on to the north, about Mons, and this only ceased at 11 o'clock. Then the silence and stillness outside were most uncanny. It was a silence that could be felt.

CHAPTER XXXVIII

THE END OF IT ALL

AFTER THE ARMISTICE the Divisional observers were not disbanded at once. They remained in my charge till December 6, when orders came for us all to return to our own units. So ended the most pleasant command that I held during the war.

The men who were with me when we were disbanded, were:

Observers (7th N.F.)

- L.-C. Cowen
- Pte. King, M.M.
- Pte. Fail
- Pte. Ewart
- Pte. Drake
- Pte. Addinall
- Pte. Austin
- Pte. Greenwood (10th M.R.)
- Pte. Firth (6th M.R.)

Signallers (7th N.F.)

- L.-C. Crozier, M.M.
- Pte. Ward
- Pte. Robinson
- Pte. Parkin

From the nature of the organisation and equipment of Infantry observers, they were of more use during trench warfare than moving warfare. You cannot turn an observer into a scout at a moment's notice. Only a few of the men ever acquired any real knowledge of map reading - they did not take the same interest in it as in other parts of the training - and for moving warfare it is absolutely essential. Another handicap was lack of transport, we were nobody's children and left to fend for ourselves. The Q.M. of the 7th N.F. adopted us so far as rations were concerned, but the collection of rations alone prevented us from being a really mobile force: we could not move far away from the source of food supplies.

During the ten weeks on the Auchonvillers Ridge the men did wonders. But we never stayed long enough at the same place after that to give them a real chance; and they never settled down to moving warfare.

On December 6 I was attached to B Company of the 7th N.F., commanded by Major Smail, and living at Boussières; once more I became a platoon commander, after nearly three years of continuous warfare.

About December 15 the 42nd Division moved into Belgium, and D.H.Q. were established at Charleroi. After arriving here I became Demobilisation Officer for the 7th N.F. and continued at that till January 19.[20] Then I went on leave to England. On February 10 I got back to Charleroi, and on February 13 I left Charleroi for demobilisation or rather 'disembodiment.' I reached home at 4.30 P.M. on February 22, glad to be back.

20. I had the greatest assistance from Cpl. Seals (7th N.F.), formerly N.C.O. in charge of Brigade Orderlies.